C0-BPU-197

THE GUSTAVE A. AND MAMIE W. EFROYMSON
MEMORIAL LECTURES
DELIVERED AT THE
HEBREW UNION COLLEGE-JEWISH INSTITUTE OF RELIGION
IN THE SPRING OF 1989

THE GUSTAVE A. AND MAMIE W. EFROYMSON
MEMORIAL LECTURES

HAIM M. I. GEVARYAHU
The Theology and Biblical Scholarship of
Yehezkel Kaufmann

ARNALDO MOMIGLIANO
Aspects of Judaism from the Hellenic and the Roman Angle

ELIEZER SCHWEID
Jewish Survival in Exile: An Israeli View

BERNARD LEWIS
The Jews of Islam

GEORGE L. MOSSE
German Jews Beyond Judaism

DAVID WINSTON
Logos and Mystical Theology in Philo of Alexandria

ARTHUR GREEN
Devotion and Commandment:
The Faith of Abraham in the Hasidic Imagination

PETER GAY
A Godless Jew:
Freud, Atheism, and the Making of Psychoanalysis

LOUIS JACOBS
God, Torah, Israel:
Traditionalism Without Fundamentalism

ROBERT ALTER
Kafka, Scholem, Benjamin:
Tradition and the Quandaries of Modernity

God, Torah, Israel

Traditionalism Without Fundamentalism

LOUIS JACOBS

HEBREW UNION COLLEGE PRESS

Cincinnati

BM
601
.J27
1990

Copyright 1990 by the Hebrew Union College Press
Hebrew Union College-Jewish Institute of Religion

Library of Congress Cataloging-in-Publication Data

Jacobs, Louis.
    God, Torah, Israel : traditionalism without fundamentalism / Louis
Jacobs.
        p. cm.
    Includes bibliographical references.
    ISBN 0-87820-052-5
    1. Judaism—Doctrines. 2. God (Judaism) 3. Revelation (Jewish
theology) 4. Jews—Election, Doctrine of. 5. Judaism and science.
I. Title.
BM601.J27 1990
296.3—dc20   90-30238
                                                                  CIP

Manufactured in the United States of America
Distributed by Behrman House, Inc.
235 Watchung Avenue, West Orange, New Jersey 07052

Contents

Preface   *vii*

Belief in a Personal *GOD*
The Position of Liberal Supernaturalism   1

TORAH as Divine Revelation
Is the Doctrine Still Acceptable to Moderns?   21

The Concept of *ISRAEL* as Chosen
The Struggle between Particularism and Universalism
Related Eschatological Questions   55

Summary   81

Notes   83

For Dr. Ian Gordon
Faithful Physician and Good Friend

Preface

IT WAS WITH a considerable degree of trepidation that I agreed, at the kind invitation of the Efroymson Committee, to deliver three lectures on the kind of theme of which the talmudic Rabbis suggest silence is golden. That I did, nevertheless, undertake this daunting task was in obedience to that other talmudic advice on etiquette: "Do not be diffident when great men invite you." The resultant lectures are now presented in print, with fairly extensive footnotes, although the form of verbal communication has been preserved wherever possible.

The position adopted in these lectures is somewhat akin to what German Jewish scholars have called "Orthopraxy" rather than "Orthodoxy" and is that adopted more or less by the Breslau school. I have tried to show, however, that such a position should not result in the attitude that one may believe what one likes as long as the mitzvot are observed. Behaviorism is no substitute for theological thinking. To believe what one likes is a purely emotional response in which the truth content of faith is ignored. A better formulation is to be open to new knowledge and to base one's belief on this openness without it leading to a negative stance towards the mitzvot. Hence I subtitle these lectures "Traditionalism Without Fundamentalism."

My thesis in these lectures is that the basic components of Judaism—God, the Torah, and Israel—are best accepted in their traditional formulations and have far greater significance for Jewish religious life in such a framework. On the other hand, I do not believe the Jewish tradition to be infallible. Obviously, in the light of modern thought, whole areas of the tradition require radical revision if congruity with the rest of our present-day knowledge is to be maintained, to say nothing of the question of whether there is such a concept as *the* Jewish tradition, a "normative Judaism" at the bar of which all truth and all values are obliged to stand. My attempt is to explore the parameters of reinterpretation and to define how far one may step before one proceeds outside Judaism altogether and virtually adopts a different religious philosophy.

Every Jewish theologian, reflecting on how the challenges to his faith are to be met, must achieve a balance between the truth claims of both the old and the new. He is helped by a kind of consensus that has emerged among committed Jews throughout the ages. With regard to Christianity and Islam, for example, it is the consensus of the believing community that has refused to allow anyone to suggest that Judaism's daughter religions can ever be seen as Judaism through a process of reinterpretation. It is acknowledged that while Jews for Jesus may still retain their halakhic status as Jews, by no stretch of the imagination can they be considered Jews professing the Jewish religion. On another level, I argue that to understand Judaism in naturalistic terms—in which God is the name given to the force that makes for righteousness, in which the Torah is a totally human composition, and in which the Jewish people is not chosen because there is no personal God to do the choosing—is similarly to go beyond the legitimate boundaries of a traditional Jewish theology. Nowadays, however, there is no clear consensus in this matter. Many religious Jews have opted for naturalism and consider the supernaturalistic approach to be reactionary or bordering on the superstitious. Nonetheless, I defend religious supernaturalism, which, I believe, is gradually coming into its own again after its partial eclipse and which to me is the most cogent and convincing picture of Judaism, superior both logically and theologically to its naturalistic rival.

A special difficulty attends on delivering theological lectures in an institute of higher Jewish learning. Not a trace of dogmatism need or should arise in a lecture of pure Jewish scholarship. One can safely leave aside one's own predilections when discussing the structure of the talmudic *sugya* or the historical Baal Shem Tov. A lecturer on topics such as these is not required to be personally involved. He need not accept the binding religious nature of the Talmud in the first instance, and there is certainly no need for him to be a Hasid in the second. If he has the knowledge to tackle these subjects, he need not be a Jew at all in order to carry his arguments to a successful conclusion. Theology, on the other hand, by its very nature demands personal commitment. The theologian not only describes what his coreligionists have believed in the past; he proclaims what he personally believes as a current member of the faith community. Complete objectivity is neither possible nor desirable in this area. I must consequently declare at the outset that I believe in religious supernaturalism and am not acting as an advocate for a case I am really convinced is weak. I shall do my best to be fair to the other side and even try to be objective, while trying not to delude myself that such objectivity is entirely possible in matters upon which persons of good will on both sides have strong opinions.

My thanks are due to the Hebrew Union College Press for the great care with which they have seen my book through to publication. I am especially grateful to Barbara Selya for her excellent copyediting and sympathetic understanding.

Belief in a Personal *GOD*
The Position of Liberal Supernaturalism

AT THE BEGINNING of this century in the United States, debate raged furiously in Protestant circles between liberals and fundamentalists. The liberals, accepting the findings of biblical criticism and the conclusions of modern science, held that the Bible could no longer be seen as completely accurate and infallible and that, consequently, the whole question of divine inspiration needed to be reconsidered in the light of the new knowledge. The fundamentalists retorted that the inerrancy of Scripture is a *fundamental*, to jettison which is to abandon the faith completely. In traditional Judaism, this position takes a slightly different turn: It has been argued that there cannot be a Jewish fundamentalism since traditional Judaism does not take the Bible literally; this is a mere quibble, however, in that then the rabbinic interpretation is adopted in a fundamentalistic way. Unless you believe, Jewish fundamentalists declare, that God conveyed directly to Moses that interpretation of the Bible found in rabbinic literature, you might as well reject Judaism in toto. For reasons to be considered in the lecture on Torah, most modern Jews reject this understanding of revelation. But it by no means follows that those who accept the liberal approach to revelation cannot believe in a God who reveals Himself. I shall argue that there is nothing in modern thought to demand the rejection of the traditional theistic view that God is a real Being, involved in nature but other than and beyond nature. *Liberal*

3

supernaturalism is that attitude which affirms the being and transcendence of a personal God while remaining open to the fresh insights regarding the manner in which God becomes manifest in the universe He has created.[1]

Israel Zangwill once said of the ancient Rabbis that while they were the most religious of men they had no word for religion. Of the Jewish religious thinkers in the premodern age (before the French Revolution and Jewish Emancipation), it can similarly be said that, while they undoubtedly believed in a personal God, they had no word for "person." To be sure, the medieval thinkers, in particular, had a highly sophisticated and extremely abstract conception of the Deity: they preferred, in Pascal's famous terminology, "the God of the philosophers" to "the God of Abraham, Isaac and Jacob." For all their stress on God's ineffability, however, they too believed that God really *is*. As the medieval thinkers — Jewish, Christian and Moslem alike — discussed God in the vocabulary they had adopted from the Greeks, He is both transcendent and immanent, in space and time and yet beyond space and time, His essence defying any attempt at comprehension, yet capable of human apprehension through His manifestation, the glory of which fills the universe. Of course, no one who thinks of God as a person is unaware that personhood is associated with the human condition and is totally inappropriate when applied to God; but then, so is all human language. The description of God as personal is meant to imply that there is a Being (this term, too, is totally inadequate) by whom we were brought into existence and whom we encounter and who encounters us. To affirm that God is a person, or, better, not less than a person, is to affirm that He is more than a great idea the emergence of which, like the invention of the wheel and of writing and the discovery of electricity, has shaped civilization.[2]

What are the causes of the decline in theistic belief — that is, belief in a personal God? Ever since the Renaissance, human ingenuity has tended to replace a God-centered universe with a universe the center of which is man. The existence of God has, as a consequence, not been so much denied as it has been considered increasingly irrelevant to a world which is constantly reminded of *mankind's* impressive achievements in art, literature, music, science, and technology. At the same time, the religious mind, always in need of the transcendence that only theism can satisfy, has begun to be haunted by a terrible question: What if theism, desirable though it may be, is not true? Once Darwin offered an explanation of how species developed by the process of natural selection, once astronomers uncovered the vastnesses of a universe in which our whole solar system is no more than a speck in outer space, once Marx pointed to the economic motivation behind religious belief and Freud to the possibility that religion is a collective neurosis, belief in the God who cares for each individual has become highly problematical.[3]

Some religious thinkers, notably Paul Tillich and the "Death of God" theologians on the Christian scene, Mordecai Kaplan and his Reconstructionist school on the Jewish, reluctant to allow victory to the bleak philosophy of atheism, have argued that the only way to meet the challenge is to give up not the idea of theism but the understanding of God as a divine person. Yes, these thinkers concede, after Darwin and the others, it is impossible to believe in the God who creates and fashions, who intervenes in the affairs of the universe, who loves His creatures and listens to their prayers, who can endow the human soul with immortality, and who can guarantee that evil will ultimately be vanquished. That personal God, they maintain, is dead because, we now see, He never existed in the first place. But if God is understood as the power in the universe that makes for righteousness, if belief in God means that, by faith, we affirm that the universe is so constituted that goodness will ultimately win out, then God, far from being dead, is truly alive, the most vital reality for the enrichment and ennoblement of human life.[4]

For Jewish thinkers who espouse this doctrine of naturalism, prayer and ritual are still of the highest value.[5] Prayer is not, however, an exercise in trying to beseech an undecided deity to grant our desires; it is, rather, a reaching out to the highest in the universe and in ourselves. In the life of prayer, our attention is called to the eternal values and this, in itself, makes their realization in our lives more feasible. Similarly, the Jewish rituals are still mitzvot and serve the same purpose as prayer. They link our individual strivings to the strivings of the Jewish people towards the fullest realization of the Jewish spirit. Even for the naturalist, then, the mitzvot are divine commands, but these commands arise from the experiences of the Jewish people in its long collective trek through history rather than as the dictates of a divine lawgiver.

This attitude should be treated with respect: In the past it has saved many Jews from abandoning a religious outlook on life, and many today still find it the only tenable approach to Judaism in the modern world. It cuts across the usual divisions in Jewish life, with devotees in the Orthodox as well as in the Conservative and Reform movements — though Orthodox Jews are less likely to admit openly to it. The trouble with religious naturalism, however, is that it does not deliver what it promised, a God capable of being worshiped. How can a vague belief that there is a mindless something "out there" be a real substitute for the traditional theistic belief that there is Mind behind and in the universe? The appeal of theism in its traditional form lies precisely in this, that the universe makes sense because it has an Author who continues to guide and watch over His creatures. The traditional argument for the existence of God — pointing to the evidence of order and design in the universe as proof that there is a Master Designer — provides powerful support for the liberal supernaturalist's position but has no weight at all as an argument for naturalism.[6] Indeed, how can one sustain the conviction that there really exists the supposed power that makes for righteousness in the world when, based on the naturalistic premise itself, that power is mindless?

The advocates of religious naturalism, influenced by science, appear to imagine that to describe God as an impersonal force or power is more philosophically respectable today than to think of Him as a person. Is it? As the medieval thinkers never tired of saying, all human descriptions of God are really inadmissible; yet since the object of worship, to be worshiped, has to produce some picture in the mind, it is necessary to use halting human language, the only language we have, always with the proviso that the reality is infinitely more than anything we dare utter. We must perforce use in our description terms taken from the highest in our experience and then add "and infinitely more than this." A force or power, precisely because it is impersonal and hence mindless, is inferior in every way to the human personality. To use the demolition job done by the scientists as a reason for preferring the force or power metaphor is to overlook the obvious fact that scientists themselves operate through their human minds. Of course, from one point of view, it is absurd to speak of God as a *person*, a term laden with all too human associations. But it is even more absurd to speak of God as an *It*, which is what speaking of Him as a force or power involves. William Temple was on surer grounds, philosophically and religiously, when he said that to speak of God as *He* is to say that *He* is more than a *He* but not less. An *It*, however, is less than a *He*.

Here it can be objected, is not to take such a position to ignore the real challenges that have been presented to traditional theism? Is it not a cowardly retreat into fundamentalism? No so. Your fundamentalist does not face the challenge: He simply denies that there is one. For him, the evolutionists were wrong; the findings of the astronomers were known all along to the Rabbis; Freud's contention that religion has its origin in the irrational fears of primitive man was an "illusion," as is the notion that there has ever been such a creature as primitive man. The liberal supernaturalist, on the other hand, has an open mind on the question of how the idea of God came into the human mind and will be prepared to acknowledge that often a religious outlook is no more than wishful thinking. He will, moreover, make the additional distinction between the question of whether God exists and the very different question, If God exists, what are the mechanics He uses? On the question of the mechanics, for example, Darwin and Freud may well be right. Who are we to say that God, in His infinite wisdom, did not choose these and other great thinkers as His instruments to convey to other humans the way in which He works?

The failure to consider both of these questions has led to a soulless scienticism. Freud, for example, was convinced that God does not exist and that religion is an illusion. Since there is no God, Freud asked, how did the idea that there is one come into the human mind? And since belief in God is an illusion, why does it persist among the human race? That the theist denies that there is any cogency to Freud's basic premise does not mean that he must reject the ensuing Freudian explanations. If he becomes convinced by what Freud had to say, he will go on to conclude that, thanks to Freud's insight, we now have a better understanding of how God chose to make Himself known in the infancy of the human race and how He uses man's natural fears in a hostile environment to cause man to rely on God as his sole refuge.

Rabbi A.I. Kook in his essay "The Pangs of Cleansing" holds that the believer ought not to be too disturbed by attacks on his belief. These attacks are often directed against crude notions of deity which all but the most naive believers do not themselves entertain. When believers are tempted to adopt unworthy and unrefined ideas about God, the atheistic attacks, by exposing the crudities, pull the believers back.[7] This *via negativa*, the negation from the idea of God of anthropomorphic associations, has respectable antecedents in Jewish thought, and we can now look at these. What must be said at the outset, however, is that the way of negation is very different from the reductionism of the religious naturalists. The way of negation affirms that we know nothing and can say nothing about God's essence. At the same time, however, it also affirms that the unknown God can be apprehended in His manifestation. For the reductionist, on the other hand, what the supernaturalist sees as God's manifestation *is* God — that is to say, there is no Being manifesting Himself in creation.

Maimonides and other medieval thinkers have developed the idea of negative attributes. Regarding God's essential attributes, those of existence, wisdom, and unity, one can only speak in negative terms. Thus to say that God exists is not to say anything about His actual nature for that is unknowable. All it means — a very big *all* — is that He is not nonexistent, that there really is an unknowable God. Similarly, to say that God is wise is to say that whatever else He is He is not ignorant. And to say that He is One is to negate multiplicity from His Being.[8] There is a real difficulty here, however. Logically, what difference is there between negating a negation and a positive affirmation? The two are surely the same. It would seem that the issue for the medieval thinkers is not so much a matter of semantics as it is a matter of psychological need.[9] To pray to God, the worshiper must have some picture of God in his mind. As we have argued, the most effective picture is drawn from human personality, the most significant construct available to man in his universe. But the picture in the mind must never be accepted as the reality; the mental reservation must always be present. As the famous Kabbalist Moses Cordovero puts it: "The mind of the worshiper must run to and fro, running to affirm that God is (and for this the picture is essential) and then immediately recoiling lest the mental picture be imagined to be all that is affirmed."[10]

The Kabbalists speak of God as He is in Himself as *En Sof*, "That which has no limits."[11] Of this aspect of deity nothing at all can be said. Even the way of negation is impermissible when applied to *En Sof*. This does not mean that the Kabbalists believe in two gods, one revealed, the other hidden. *Deus abs-conditus* is *Deus revelatus.*

The liberal supernaturalist will not, of course, consider himself necessarily bound to accept the formulations of Maimonides or of the Kabbalists. Because he has a liberal approach, he will tend to see these and similar formulations in historical terms — that is, as conditioned by the thought patterns of the age in which the particular thinkers lived. What he gains from their speculations is the appreciation that the true nature of God is bound to be a mystery beyond the grasp of the human mind. As the sage quoted by Albo has it: "If I knew Him I would be He."[12] That there has been a considerable degree of freedom in the Jewish tradition to speculate on the mystery is comforting to the liberal supernaturalist, who is thus encouraged to engage in his own speculations. But because he believes in the God of the tradition (the speculations and the freedom to speculate are themselves part of that tradition), he will always stop short of reductionism. He will steadfastly refuse to refine God out of existence, so to speak.

There are thus three attitudes on the question of God for the modern Jew: He can be an atheist, he can be a religious naturalist, or he can be a religious supernaturalist. In other words, he can deny that God exists, he can reinterpret the idea of God in terms of the force or power that makes for righteousness, or he can believe in the personal God of the Jewish tradition. It all depends on which attitude makes the most sense of human life and is the most coherent philosophy of existence. One man's coherence is another's incoherence. Subjectivity is no doubt an element in the choice for all three philosophies. This is presumably what Kierkegaard and the other religious existentialists refer to when they speak of "the leap of faith," a rather over-worked concept in contemporary Jewish religious thought but useful in calling attention to this element of freely choosing one's philosophy. Let us examine briefly why the liberal supernaturalist prefers this attitude to the other two.

To think of God as a person is first to justify coherence itself. For if, as the atheist maintains, the universe is just there as brute fact, and if, as the religious naturalist maintains, the force that works for righteousness is similarly just there, how does one explain that feature of coherence in the universe by which science operates—indeed, by which all human reasoning operates? Taylor's famous illustration is germane in this connection.[13] In some English railway stations near the Welsh border, small pebbles are arranged to form the words "Welcome to Wales." A skeptical passenger in the railway carriage may decide that, somehow, the pebbles just happened to have gotten there, coincidentally, to form these words by accident. What that skeptic cannot reasonably do, based on his perception, is to turn to his fellow passengers and inform them that they are entering Wales. The liberal supernaturalist would not mistake the welcome sign for an accidental formation of pebbles, but neither does he attempt to explain everything in this strange and mysterious universe, which he believes has been created by a benevolent Mind. He cannot understand why there is evil in the universe, for instance. But he can explain why humans have this constant urge to explain, the human mind exploring the workings of Infinite Mind behind the universe. In the other two hypotheses, all is random development. But randomness implies that all is fortuitous and coincidental so that ultimately there is no meaning to meaning. Unless there is a personal God, whence came personality? Unless there is Mind behind the universe, whence came human reasoning powers? Unless righteousness is written large in the universe, whence came the power that makes for righteousness—indeed, whence came the very concept of righteousness? If everything just happened to be, it would not only be religion that was wishful thinking. All thinking would be wishful.

The poet bravely and stoically declares:

It fortifies my soul to know
That though I perish truth is so.

But without belief in God in the traditional sense, what *is* this soul fortified by the truth? And where and what is that truth that those poor souls who are doomed to perish may proclaim it? Similarly, when W.E. Henley rejoices in his "unconquerable soul," he has to offer his thanks to "whatever gods may be." Ultimately, there is no escaping the "Hound of Heaven." Faith in reason is ultimately faith in God; faith in goodness is ultimately faith in God.

The Christian understanding of theism is, with few exceptions, to stress that God is personal. Indeed, in the classical Christian doctrine of the Trinity, there are three persons in the Godhead. Jews, naturally, have rejected the Christian dogma as incompatible with pure monotheism. And while the Jewish supernaturalist takes issue with the naturalistic idea because it is too impersonal, he rejects the Christian idea because it is too personal. In his polemic against Christianity, the seventeenth-century Venetian Rabbi, Leon Modena, is not convinced that the doctrine of the Trinity per se is totally incompatible with the Jewish position. He points out that the Kabbalistic doctrine of the *Sefirot*, the ten powers or potencies in the Godhead through which *En Sof* becomes manifest, resembles, to some extent, the Christian Trinity.[14] (Even though the Kabbalists were devout Jews, opponents of the Kabbalah accused them of being, as they put it, "worse than the Christians" in that the Kabbalists spoke of ten, rather than three, aspects of the divine unity.)[15] It is the affirmation of the three *persons* in the Trinity that has made Christianity offensive to Jews—specially the Christian doctrine of the Incarnation in which one of the three assumes human flesh. The author of an article in the journal *Judaism* a few years ago maintained that Jews have not argued against the doctrine of the Incarnation because of the impossibility of God assuming human form, but only because this did not, in fact, happen.[16] Such a position is absurd. Jews have held that God, being God, cannot assume human flesh. In the Jewish doctrine, it is as impossible for God to do so as it is for Him to deny Himself or to wish Himself out of existence. Contradiction, as Aquinas said, does not fall under the scope of divine omnipotence. The sober fact is that Jews throughout the ages have held the Christian doctrine to be idolatrous and have laid down their lives rather than embrace Christianity, although some Jewish teachers have qualified this by stating that Christianity is an idolatrous faith for "us" — that is for Jews, but not for "them" — that is, for Gentiles, who are enjoined by the Torah to reject idolatry, but who do not offend against the Noachide Laws by adopting the Christian faith.[17]

The Jewish supernaturalist obviously rejects agnosticism as he rejects atheism. The term agnosticism, which was coined by T.H. Huxley in the last century, was intended to convey the idea that there can be no "gnosis," no knowledge, about God.[18] He was not saying, as many agnostics do nowadays, that he could not decide whether or not God exists, but rather that since the whole subject is not amenable to proof, it is *impossible* to decide one way or the other. There is thus a "hard" and a "soft" agnosticism. The "hard" agnostic holds that one can never know whether or not God exists. The "soft" agnostic cannot make up his mind on the question. The fallacy in the "soft" option is that belief in God profoundly affects a person's life, the whole quality of which is different from the life of the atheist. As Chesterton rightly said: "Show me a man's philosophy and I'll show you the man." One can adopt an agnostic attitude towards certain questions with little consequence: one can, for example, live perfectly well without ever knowing whether there are intelligent beings on other planets. But a man and a woman may agonize for a lifetime over whether they really love one another and thus never marry. And by leaving the matter in abeyance, by not deciding whether or not he believes in God, the agnostic, in fact, has decided to live without God. To remain undecided all of one's life, then, is, in effect, to decide against.

As for "hard" agnosticism, it is difficult to understand on what grounds it is affirmed that one can never know whether or not God exists. How does the agnostic *know* that he can never know? All the pros and cons have been presented to him. Why should the human mind be incapable of deciding one way or the other on this question as it decides on other questions?

For all that, the liberal supernaturalist, while ruling out agnosticism on the basic question of God's existence, may well adopt an attitude of reverent or religious agnosticism on other questions. Because of his liberal stance, he will weigh dogma in the light of history and of reason and may come up with views that are less traditional but more coherent to him in the light of new knowledge; or he may feel that the problem is too complicated for a tidy *yes* or *no* to be given and must be left to God.

Finally, we must consider the idea of a limited personal God. Among many other thinkers, Gersonides in the Middle Ages, John Stuart Mill,[19] E.S. Brightman,[20] and Charles Hartshorne[21] in modern times, have presented a view of theism in which the idea of God's omnipotence is qualified. Saadiah Gaon, in his *Beliefs and Opinions*[22] argued, as did Aquinas centuries later,[23] that God, who can do that which is impossible for us to do, cannot do that which is logically impossible. For instance, says Saadiah, God cannot pass the whole world through a signet ring without making either the world smaller or the ring larger. Actually, here it is not a question of whether God can or cannot do something. The statement "To pass the whole world through a ring without making the world smaller or the ring larger," is a self-contradictory and hence logically meaningless jumble of words. To pass A through B means that B is larger than A so that the statement is as logically meaningless as "to make the world smaller or the ring larger without making the world smaller or the ring larger." When one asks questions of this kind, one is really asking "Can God. . .?" without completing the sentence.

The doctrine of omnipotence, however, can be qualified in still other ways. There is the classic problem of predetermination, for example. Gersonides, bothered by the old question of how God's foreknowledge is compatible with human freedom, holds that what God knows beforehand is all the choices open to each individual; He does not know, however, which choice the individual, in his freedom, will make.[24] Other thinkers similarly qualify God's omnipotence. God has all the power there is, but He is limited by what is called "The Given," that is, by things as they are. Such ideas are not a form of dualism, a belief in two gods. In dualism there are two powers, one good, the other evil, contending for supremacy: that view is certainly incompatible with Jewish monotheism. In the idea of God as personal but limited, He has no rival; there is only One God who is all powerful in some respects but lacking a degree of power in other respects because that is how things are.

Take the problem of evil, often expressed in the form: Either God can prevent evil and does not choose to do so, in which case He cannot be good. Or he wishes to prevent evil but cannot do so, in which case He cannot be omnipotent. An answer often given is that God does have the power to banish evil but does not do so because in some way evil serves the cause of good; for example, a universe in which there was no evil would be a universe in which freedom to choose the good would be impossible.[25] Exponents of the limited God idea, however, see no dilemma. God is good and would prevent evil if He could but He cannot. He is not, in fact, omnipotent, and evil is simply there. Of course God can and does mitigate the banefulness of evil, and He can and does urge His creatures to fight evil and be on the side of good.

Although I find this whole notion incoherent, it is possible for a supernaturalist Jew to adopt such a position without finding himself outside of Judaism. On a surface reading of the Jewish tradition, the picture which emerges is indeed one of God struggling, as it were, with that in the universe which frustrates His will. Gersonides, in his work *The Wars of the Lord* (in which he puts forward his view on God's limited foreknowledge) holds that only such a view does complete justice to the biblical record. The abstract term "omnipotence," after all, was coined by thinkers influenced by Greek thought. Neither the term nor the idea of an *all*-powerful God is found in the Bible or in the rabbinic sources. In the Lurianic Kabbalah, the first stage in the divine creative processes is that of *tzimtzum*, the withdrawal of *En Sof* "from Himself into Himself" in order to make room, as it were, for the finite universe. Thus, in this view, the universe could only have come into existence through God's self-limitation, through His allowing finitude to encroach on His Infinity; thus, there is a doctrine of a limited God in manifestation, though not in essence, in this theology of Judaism. In an even more radical version of the Lurianic Kabbalah, *En Sof* purges Himself of the evil within Himself by His withdrawal to leave room for the universe. This version of the Kabbalah is careful to stress that the evil was only present in infinitesimal quantity, "like a grain of salt in a vast ocean."[26]

For all the attempts of some to rename Gersonides' work "Wars *Against* the Lord" the limited God idea, unlike atheism, agnosticism, dualism, and the doctrine of the Trinity, is not necessarily incompatible with monotheism as understood by Judaism. The question is not, however, Is the idea Jewish? but rather, Is it convincing?

Isaac Husik dubbed Gersonides' idea that God does not know the contingent "a theological monstrosity."[27] That might be an overstatement, but every radical qualification of the idea of God's power results in severe theological difficulties, even if it is otherwise philosophically attractive. The problem with the notion of "The Given," for example, is that it is extremely difficult to entertain the notion of a God who has to work with poor material not of His own making. And what is to become of the whole idea of a purposeful God if, by definition, He can know the future only in general terms and does not know the particular choices individuals will make—choices which may very well result in the frustration of His purpose. To reply that, indeed, God depends on His creatures for the fulfillment of His purpose is to turn God into a divine experimenter and that, surely, is a distortion of the Jewish faith, popular though the notion might be with the poetic mind. This is very different from the typically Jewish idea that God *uses* His creatures as coworkers for the realization of a purpose He knows will ultimately be realized.

A different and even more radical understanding of the personhood of God is provided in some versions of Hasidic thought, in which God is not a Being totally above His creatures but the One who embraces the All in the fullness of His Being. This notion is best called panentheism, "all is in God," though the Hasidim themselves used no such abstract term for their doctrine. In this view, from God's point of view, as it were, only God enjoys ultimate existence. It is only from the point of view of God's creatures that they and the universe they inhabit enjoy existence independently of God.[28] If by a "Jewish" doctrine is meant a doctrine held by Jews, then Hasidic panentheism is undoubtedly Jewish — although opponents of Hasidism like the Gaon of Vilna believed the notion to be rank heresy.[29] That the Vilna Gaon declared it to be heresy would not make it such for the liberal supernaturalist but here, too, there are severe difficulties, chief of which is, how can it be said that the universe and its creatures only enjoy existence from their point of view and not from God's point of view? Either they exist or do not exist.

In this lecture we have tried to consider the meaning of the doctrine of a personal God and have contrasted it with rival theological formulations. I have argued that liberal supernaturalism is both the closest in approximation to the traditional Jewish view, or, at least, to the implications of that view, and that it scores over its rivals in its coherence. The mystery remains, however, and, God being God, must remain. It was a religious man who composed the salutory doggerel:

Dear God, for as much as without Thee
We are not even able to doubt Thee.
Lord give us the grace
To convince the whole race
We know nothing whatever about Thee.

God, Torah, Israel

This takes us to the heart of the matter. The sophisticated theist can address God as *Thou* and can pray to Him and yet, in that very prayer, admit, as he must, that God is unknowable. But there is all the difference in the world between the ineffability of God as conceived of by the theist and the mysterious force that makes for righteousness of the religious naturalist. In the former, the true nature of God cannot be uttered or known by the human mind because God is too great to be encapsulated in human expression. In the latter, all that is affirmed is that somehow we live in the faith that the universe is so constituted that goodness will ultimately win out. No theist will seek to deny that there are difficulties in the theistic position. If he, nonetheless, opts for theism against atheism or agnosticism it is because theism, for all its difficulties, makes more sense of the universe and of human life. It is this "making sense" that is the appeal of theism. The mystery lies in the concept of the Being whom thought cannot reach; it is not a falling back on the idea of "we do not know" and leaving it at that. The whole race has to continue to live without knowing anything about God and yet countless human beings have lived and still live in the conviction that there is a *Thou* infinitely more that an *It* in charge of the universe.

While there does not seem to be any convincing midway position between theism and atheism on the theoretical level, there is, of course, an ebb and flow in the life of faith: there are times when the believer has complete conviction, other times when he is not so sure, other times again when his faith is completely shattered. But the content of belief in God does not allow for semantic confusion for the believer or the nonbeliever. All of the arguments for and against theism can be debated at length, but the discussion must not center on the meaning of the *term* God. The theist is convinced that God exists; the atheist denies it. In trying to be theist and atheist at the same time, the religious naturalist seems to be involved in semantic sleight of hand when he reduces the *term* to mean only that power that makes for

righteousness in the world. This is a very different approach
from postulating two hypothetical views of the same Being as
one does in considering the idea that God is omnipotent and the
idea that He is limited in some respects. When the religious
naturalist defends his use of the term to link his concept with
Jewish tradition, this is precisely the question: Does not such a
radical reinterpretation of theism sever that link entirely? It is no
way to meet the real challenges to belief in modern times to say
that theism is now to be understood in a different sense from
that in which it has been understood throughout history. It is
rather like saying that antisemitic allegations no longer have any
force because the people hitherto considered to be Jews are not
Jews at all. The believer in a personal God, because he is a
believer, should be ready to express his doubts and speculate on
the mystery. He may then emerge from the struggle with his
faith fortified and enriched.

TORAH as Divine Revelation
Is the Doctrine Still Acceptable to Moderns?

IN THE PREVIOUS lecture we examined the traditional theistic point of view, defending it against the attacks of the rejectionists and the revisionists. In this lecture I shall try to defend the traditional doctrine of revelation. In this area, however, a strong measure of revisionism is inevitable — that is to say, although the traditional view of the Torah as dictated by God to Moses directly has to go, this should not result in total rejection of the traditional doctrine "The Torah is from heaven" (*Torah min ha-shamayim*). First we must note the usual form in which this doctrine came to be presented (a form still accepted by Orthodoxy). Then we can try to see why a more or less drastic revision or reinterpretation of this formulation is demanded.

According to the traditional view, God conveyed the Pentateuch, the Five Books of Moses, directly and in its entirety to Moses (with the possible exception of the final verses in Deuteronomy, which speak of Moses' death[1]) during the forty years in which the Israelites journeyed through the wilderness. In addition to the Written Torah, the Pentateuch, recorded in writing by Moses, there was a series of communications conveyed to Moses during the forty days and nights he spent on Mount Sinai, in which all the details of the Law were explained to him. This latter, together with all the later elaborations found in the talmudic literature, the work of the Rabbis, is known as the Oral Torah (*Torah she-be-al peh*). Of course, the Rabbis introduced

23

new legislation from time to time; the point, however, is that the sanction for such rabbinic legislation is found in the Written Torah, which was read as giving authority to the sages of Israel to "make a fence around the Torah," so that, in a sense, rabbinic law is also biblical law.

Thus the Torah is the very word of God — the teachings, laws, doctrines and rules for the conduct of life as conveyed by the Author of life. To study the Torah is to think God's thoughts after Him. To practice the precepts, the mitzvot, of the Torah is to obey God's will. And this Torah has remained unchanged throughout the ages, conveyed, through the chain of tradition, from Moses to Joshua, from Joshua to the Elders, from the Elders to the Prophets and from the Prophets to the Men of the Great Synagogue, as stated in the opening passage of *Ethics of the Fathers*, and then by father to son, teacher to disciple, through three thousand years of Jewish history. As Maimonides formulates it in his Thirteen Articles of the Faith:

The eighth principle of faith. That the Torah has been revealed from Heaven. This implies our belief that the whole of this Torah found in our hands this day is the Torah that was handed down to Moses and that it is all of divine origin. By this I mean that the whole of the Torah came unto him from before God which is metaphorically called "speaking"; but the real nature of that communication is unknown to everyone except to Moses to whom it came. . . .And there is no difference between verses like "And the sons of Ham were Cush and Mizraim, Phut and Canaan" [Gen. 10:6], or "And his wife's name was Mehetabel, daughter of Matred" [Gen. 36:39], or "And Timna was concubine" [Gen. 36:12], and verses like "I am the Lord thy God" [Exod. 20:2] and "Hear, O Israel" [Deut. 6:4]. They are all equally of divine origin and all belong to "The Law of God which is perfect, pure, holy and true.". . .The interpretation of traditional law is in like manner of divine origin. And that which we know today of the nature of Sukkah, Lulab, Shofar, Tzitzit and Tefillin is essentially the same as that which God commanded Moses, and which the latter told us.[2]

In such a view, there is no room for any notion of development in the Jewish religion: the Torah is a static body of truth handed down intact from generation to generation. Maimonides' formulation may seem extreme, if not to say, rigid, but, in one form or another, this view was accepted until modern times by all Jews loyal to rabbinic Judaism. Even the Karaites held fast to the doctrine that every word of the Pentateuch was dictated by God to Moses, although they took issue with the doctrine of the Oral Torah, which they held to be rabbinic invention. I have used the word *dictated*. Although this is perhaps the best word to use for the traditional view, thinkers like Maimonides would not have been happy with it because the notion it suggests is far too crude. Maimonides is careful to speak of divine communication as a process that only Moses himself, the recipient of that communication, could understand.

Thus, the traditional picture has grandeur and power. The Infinite has communicated to the people of Israel, and through them, albeit in a less demanding way, to all mankind, how life should be lived. Every mitzvah is not only a means to an end but is itself the glorious end—none could be more sublime—of doing God's will. That is why there was such strong opposition in the Middle Ages to the attempt by thinkers like Maimonides to discover the reasons for the mitzvot. Not only was such pursuit an impious questioning of the divine will. It was more serious than that. It tended to make whatever reason was discovered the end to which each mitzvah was directed. As the critics of Maimonides said, for him everything is *for* some great idea, the achievement of happiness and justice in society, for example, or the inculcation of true ideas, and nothing was a good in itself. Maimonides and other thinkers retorted that, on the contrary, to carry out the mitzvot as if they were unreasonable was to bring Judaism into disrepute, to weaken the hold of the mitzvot on the people, and, worst of all, to conceive of God as a tyrannical ruler imposing arbitrary rules on His subjects.[3] Whatever side devout Jews took in this debate, however, there was no questioning the divine origins of these commands and the Jewish obligation to fulfill them. To this day, one recites a benediction blessing and thanking God for commanding us to perform each mitzvah; and this applies not only to biblical ordinances but to rabbinic ones as well — the latter, too, having been sanctioned by the Torah and thus indirectly commanded by God. Since there is no reference to Hanukkah in the Torah, for example, the talmudic Rabbis discuss the origins of the command to kindle the Hanukkah lights, in other words, why we say ". . .who has commanded us to kindle the candle of Hanukkah."[4] The biblical source is given either as "Thou shalt not turn aside from the sentence which they shall tell thee" (Deut. 17:11), or "Ask thy father and he will show thee; thine elders and they will tell thee" (Deut. 32:7).

However binding the notion of mitzvot might have been to our forbears, however, to many Jews today the traditional view in untenable for a variety of reasons. For our purpose, the most cogent of these deserve examination.

First, the modern study of the Bible which goes by the name of Higher Criticism has succeeded in showing that the Pentateuch contains sections, at the very least, that could not possibly have been written down by Moses but must have been composed at a later date. Even some of the talmudic rabbis had argued that the last eight verses, describing Moses' death and burial, must have been written down by Joshua after the death and burial of Moses. The great twelfth-century biblical exegete Abraham Ibn Ezra extended this to the whole last section of the Pentateuch, since this passage begins, "And Moses went up. . . ." As Ibn Ezra remarks, "Once he went up he did not go down again."[5]

Ibn Ezra hinted at other anachronisms, and the Higher Critics (an unfortunate term, in that it suggests hostile scholars sitting in judgment on the Pentateuch) continued the process by noting other instances. Some passages in the Pentateuch appear to be duplicates. There are, for example, two narratives of Abraham sending away Hagar and her child, each narrative with its own vocabulary. And there are contradictions between some passages. Of the three great law codes in the Pentateuch, those in Exodus, Leviticus, and Deuteronomy, there are not only differences in content but also in style and vocabulary. Furthermore, Textual Criticism noted the differences between the standard text of the Bible, the Masoretic, and the ancient versions such as the Septuagint. While the Masoretic text is extremely reliable, it is hard to maintain that in every instance it is the only authentic text and all other versions are in error. By the nineteenth century, it had become obvious to many objective students that whoever else wrote the Pentateuch it could not have been Moses. It is extremely difficult to maintain, for example, that the oft-occurring words: "And the Lord spoke to Moses, saying. . ." were themselves "spoken" by God to Moses. Thus the Higher Critics did not ask, "Did Moses write the Pentateuch?" Instead they posed the quite different question, "Since Moses did not write the Pentateuch, who did, and when?" The consensus which has emerged as a result of this biblical scholarship is that the Pentateuch is a composite work, the parts of which were produced in different periods and then combined by an editor or editors.

But it has not only been textual research which has assailed traditional belief in *Torah min ha-shamayim:* Geologists demonstrated the immense age of the earth, astronomers that the universe is not geocentric, anthropologists that human beings have been on earth far longer by hundreds of thousands of years than Genesis seems to suggest—all making it increasingly difficult to believe that the Pentateuchal picture is the result of a direct divine communication and hence an infallible source providing completely accurate information on all matters.

Further, the *Jüdische Wissenschaft* movement, which arose in the nineteenth century, applied the newly developed methods of historical investigation to the Oral Torah, asking, for example, how, why, and when did the whole doctrine originate and why it was not accepted by the Sadducees and the Karaites. The whole of the talmudic literature was subjected to intense scrutiny in order to determine how rabbinic Judaism developed. And on the wider scene, the science of comparative religion sought to uncover the way in which religious institutions (and religion itself) express themselves, noting, among many other things, for example, that many religions have taboos about diet and suggesting that the origin of the dietary laws of the Torah may have originated in such taboos.

So the modern Jew, who lives after all this massive historical, philological and comparative work has been done (and is being done with ever greater confidence and with ever more refined methods) is faced with a severe challenge to his traditional view of *Torah min ha-shamayim*. Instead of the notion of a static transmission of a corpus of revealed truth, one now sees human beings reaching out to God, engaged in a process of trial and error, and influenced by the civilizations in which they live. Instead of the view that the Rabbis were part of an authentic tradition of interpretation reaching back to Moses and through him to God, it has come to be seen that this tradition itself is the result of the sages of Israel reflecting on the meaning of divine revelation. The secularists resolve this disparity by rejecting the religious hypothesis entirely. For them, the new picture only serves to convince them that there is no truth in the Jewish religion. But religious Jews, convinced that a surrender of religion is impossible, that the God of Israel is still the living God, continue to grapple with the problem of divine revelation. For them, three different attitudes have emerged. Many maintain simply that the new picture is wrong and is no more than an heretical misunderstanding it is right and proper to reject. Others maintain that, indeed, there is clearly a human element in the Torah and that this requires a complete reinterpretation of the tradition. The third view, the one I am trying to expound in this lecture, is that it is possible and desirable to be totally committed to Jewish observance and to treat the mitzvot as divine commands without any sacrifice of intellectual integrity.

The fundamentalist view, that nothing has changed and no departure from the medieval stance is required, can only be adopted by a wholesale rejection of all modern knowledge and scholarship. For the Jewish fundamentalist, the world is only 5,750 years old, the Higher Critics were antisemites whose sole aim was the denigration of Judaism and the Jewish people, and the Jewish historians who suggest that Judaism is a developing religion are at best misguided, at worst traitorous heretics.

To be fair, some Jewish fundamentalists do not go quite so far in rejecting all modern thought. On the question of the Genesis creation narrative versus science, for example, they do not argue that the six days of creation are actually six days and that God placed the fossils there for reasons of His own. Instead, many fall back on the suggestion, first made in the last century, that the "days" of Genesis are vast periods of time and that the "dust of the earth," out of which God created Adam, could mean the primeval swamps out of which the lowest forms of life emerged to begin the process through which man evolved. The most sophisticated statement of this position was made by Rabbi Kook, who argued that, in the Jewish tradition, the creation narrative has always been considered as belonging to the "secrets of the Torah" and hence need not be taken literally.[6] But, in this view, what is one to make of the days and *nights* of the Genesis narrative? And can the biblical word "day" really mean what it means nowhere else in the Bible, a vast period of time? And what of the evidence of human civilizations existing long before the biblical date for Adam? And what of the evidence for paleolithic and neolithic man? It is hardly necessary to resurrect the old controversy. All the attempts at establishing the idea of biblical infallibility have long been satisfactorily refuted in the view of people with open minds.

On the question of biblical criticism, it is no doubt true that some of the Critics were, indeed, motivated by a dislike of or even a hatred for Judaism and the Jews. But the whole point of the new methods is that their conclusions are subjected to examination and criticism by other workers in the field so that the new "scientific" picture that has emerged enjoys a high degree of plausibility. One may disagree with the motivation of the Critics, and even with their hypotheses: That, as many Critics still maintain, the Pentateuch consists of the four documents J, E, D and P, with a Redactor called R, may well be open to question and has, in fact, been considerably revised. But that we can safely go back to the traditional view, that the Pentateuch is of Mosaic authorship in its entirety and is in no way a composite work, is as unlikely as any hypothesis based on extreme implausibility.

Further, it cannot be overlooked that all the other books of the Bible have been studied with the application of the historical/ critical method to yield very convincing conclusions on questions of authorship, dating, and composition — conclusions that are often at variance with the views held in a precritical age. Take the book of Psalms, traditionally attributed in its entirety to David (though he admittedly used the work of earlier authors). As Krochmal remarks, in a precritical age there seemed no incongruity in imagining King David, before the Temple had even been built, gazing into the future to see, four hundred years later, the Temple destroyed and the Levites exiled to Babylon, and to compose Psalm 137 in which the Levites refuse to sing the Lord's song in a strange land.[7] With the keener sense of history every schoolboy has nowadays, it seems so much more plausible to believe that Psalm 137 was actually composed during the Babylonian exile, that the Book of Psalms is a composite work, and that King David, the "sweet singer in Israel" inspired the works of other hymn makers so that the whole book became known as the "Psalms of David." Or take the book of Isaiah. Even Ibn Ezra long ago suggested that the second part of Isaiah, from chapter 40, must have been written by a later prophet since it speaks of the exiles returning from Babylon and mentions Cyrus by name.[8] It cannot be denied on a priori grounds that God can endow a man with such power that he is able to witness in a vision events that would not occur until 150 years after his time. But, again with a keener sense of history, the vast majority of modern scholars consider it far more plausible to suggest that the second part of the book was added to the first part and that this second part consists of a contemporary account of the events. As a matter of fact, the biblical Prophets only foretell the future in general; they are not specific regarding events yet to occur in the future. Call it guesswork, if you will, as some fundamentalists do, preferring the certainty of tradition. But, then, every hypothesis is only guesswork until, supported by evidence, it comes to enjoy a high degree of plausibility. That the traditional view is "certain" is itself an hypothesis and a far less plausible one.

And then there are the scholars today who use the historical/ critical method unreservedly so far as the rest of the Bible and the rabbinic literature are concerned. They have no qualms whatsoever in speaking of post-Davidic or even Maccabean Psalms or of a Deutero-Isaiah or of the influence of Greek and Roman culture on rabbinic institutions. They will most certainly draw the line, however, when it comes to critically investigating the Holy of Holies, the Pentateuch, the very source of the Torah. These scholars, nonfundamentalists in all other areas, adopt a fundamentalist approach to the Five Books of Moses—either positively rejecting all Higher and Textual Criticism of the Torah itself or refusing to discuss or mention such criticism, as if it does not exist. Such a position is clearly untenable and is unworthy of serious scholarship. If the critical method is used effectively in all other areas and with regard to all other sacred texts, how can it be inadmissable when applied to the Pentateuch? Moreover, the notion of *Torah min ha-shamayim* is not the claim of the Pentateuch itself, but is based on the rabbinic literature, which these scholars are prepared to examine both critically and historically. To my mind, the religious significance of sacred Scripture is not affected by considerations of how it came into being. Even those fundamentalists who hold that the traditional view of the origins of the Torah is of such supreme importance that its rejection amounts to a rejection of Judaism must admit that the rabbinic view itself has had a history and, in all probability, was advanced in reaction to the heretics who maintained that the Torah was not a sacred book but was made up by Moses. Against such views, the Rabbis used conscious hyperbole when they declared, "Whoever says even a single derivation from the Torah is not 'from heaven' is one who denies the Torah and has no share in the world to come."[9]

Another rather simplistic attempt is sometimes made by those who wish to preserve the doctrine of "Torah from heaven" even while accepting the critical view. The ploy adopted by a number of devout and observant scholars is: granted that God did not convey the Torah all at once during the forty years of the Israelites' journey through the wilderness, He did reveal it at different periods through the documents of J, E, D, and P and through the Redactor who put these together.[10] The only adjustment required in the light of modern thought is neither to the "Torah" nor to "heaven" but to the "from" in the traditional doctrine. The whole Torah is God-given in a direct fashion, exactly as Maimonides says, but the recipients were the "authors" of the various documents. Such a solution is unsatisfactory because of the contradictions in the various codes in the Pentateuch and because the ultimate source of authority in the traditional view is not the Pentateuch in itself but the Pentateuch as interpreted in the rabbinic literature. Once it is accepted that the Torah is a composite work produced in different periods in response to the particular needs of the age in which the various parts were compiled — once, in other words, the human element in the Torah is acknowledged, a contradiction is involved in postulating at the same time that the Torah was "given" to a series of passive recipients.

To make this clearer, take, for instance, the two stories of Hagar and Ishmael. In Genesis chapter 16, Abraham, at the behest of Sarah, sends Hagar away; an angel, however, speaks to Hagar to tell her to return to Abraham and she will have a son, Ishmael, by him. Then, in Genesis chapter 21, Hagar is sent away together with Ishmael. Thus in the traditional view, Hagar was sent away twice—even though the narrative makes no mention of this having happened. Moreover, in the first narrative, Hagar is described as a *shifḥah* and the Tetragrammaton is used as the divine name, whereas in the second narrative Hagar is called an *amah* and the divine name used is *elohim*. Considerations of this kind have led critics to suggest that we have here two versions, each with its own vocabulary, of the sending away. Now it is possible to dismiss the critical view and to argue that, for reasons we cannot fathom, the two sendings away were conveyed each with a different vocabulary. But if one does accept the critical view, that there are, here and elsewhere, duplicates in the Pentateuch, each from a different time and place, one cannot simply say the whole text of the Pentateuch was "dictated" by God but at different times and that there were two sendings away—that is to involve oneself in contradiction. And the same argument holds with regard to the whole critical theory of the Pentateuch as a composite work.

Thus much work remains to be done, but thanks to the massive researches of a host of scholars in various disciplines during the past 150 years, a consensus has emerged with regard to how the Torah came about, and this consensus has ruled out the fundamentalist thesis. It has come to be seen that the tremendous entity we call the Torah, comprising the Pentateuch, the rest of the Bible, the Mishnah, the Talmud—and the elaborations on all of these in Jewish thought—is not static but dynamic, the constant interaction of the divine with the human. That the Torah contains a divine element no religious supernaturalist will wish to deny. But the human element, too, is quite obviously present.

While the fundamentalist view ignores this human element, the second view to which we have alluded deemphasizes the divine element and holds that, indeed, the traditional doctrine must be completely abandoned in the name of intellectual integrity. The Bible may still be seen as an inspired work but the inspiration, they believe, has been channeled through the human psyche and colored by temperament, social background, and human reactions to events. Such an attitude shifts the emphasis from the Pentateuch to the prophetic message. It is no accident that classical Reform tended to speak of the Jewish religion as "prophetic Judaism" and to allude to the laws of the Pentateuch as "Mosaic legislation" — a bloodless expression, in Mordecai Kaplan's view. In this approach, the ritual laws tend to recede and the stress is placed on Jewish ethics as the heart of Judaism. To be sure, a good deal of the ritual is still preserved, especially the rituals of the Sabbath and festivals, but the whole concept of the mitzvah as a divine command has been considerably weakened. A ritual such as circumcision, too, still exercises a powerful hold on all Jews and is generally seen as a mitzvah. But the whole range of the Halakhah is no longer seen as a categorical imperative but rather as a matter of individual choice.

Is there a third way, a way in which both the findings of modern criticism and historical investigation and the traditional doctrine of "The Torah is from heaven" are preserved so that full justice is afforded to each? At this stage I must introduce my own personal odyssey, reluctant though I am to bestir old controversies.[11] It is now almost thirty years since the so-called "Jacobs Affair" erupted in Anglo-Jewry. Here is not the occasion to describe all the discussions, the politics, and the consequences of this local controversy, which, judging by articles and comments on it in the world press, seems to have struck a chord in circles far removed from the comparatively small Anglo-Jewish community. I shall only try to delineate the main theological issue that was at stake — an issue strictly relevant to the question of whether there is a third way to deal with the question of divine revelation.

The Anglo-Jewish community is among the most tightly structured in the world. The vast majority of congregations in England are, at least nominally, Orthodox, with the Chief Rabbi as their spiritual head. Jews' College, the institution for the

training of Orthodox rabbis and ministers, cannot appoint anyone to its faculty unless the candidate receives prior authoriza-
tion from the Chief Rabbi. Furthermore, no rabbi or minister
can be appointed to his position in any congregation under the
Chief Rabbi's jurisdiction without the Chief Rabbi's
certificate — that is, his approval of the candidate's religious
qualifications.

Over the years I had expressed in writing, in speeches, and in
sermons the view that it was possible to be "Orthodox," in the
sense of complete loyalty to Jewish observances and the
Halakhah, while accepting, at the same time, the "assured
results" of modern critical scholarship. Such an attitude was
neither original nor startling. It was, in broad outline, the position of Zacharias Frankel and the Breslau School, and of Solomon Schechter and the Conservative movement in the U.S. In
Anglo-Saxon Jewry a similar view had been advanced by Herbert
Loewe and by a number of distinguished ministers in the
"Orthodox" camp such as Simeon Singer and J. Abelson. Jews'
College has always been fortunate in having on its faculty men of
outstanding scholarly ability, distinguished practitioners of
critical/historical biblical analysis: The contributions of Adolf
Büchler, Arthur Marmorstein, Isidore Epstein (Editor of the
Soncino Talmud), H.J. Zimmels, N. Weider and others to Jew-
ish scholarship have been acknowledged throughout the world.
Moreover, biblical criticism was taught for many years at Jews'
College to those preparing for the Honours Degree in Semitics at
London University. On the other hand, the former principal of
Jews' College, M. Friedländer, in his *The Jewish Religion*,[12] and
J. H. Hertz, a former Chief Rabbi, in his *Commentary to the
Torah*[13], both attacked the Higher Criticism vehemently as
destructive of the faith. Furthermore, although, as I have said,
the Higher Criticism was part of the College's curriculum, students were given the impression that this subject, useful for
obtaining a good degree in Semitics, was not really "true" and
should not be seriously entertained when they eventually gradu-

ated as rabbis or ministers. Thus there was considerable ambigu-
ity in this matter, the general tendency being to leave well
enough alone. The ship of Anglo-Jewry sailed happily along
with not a threatening cloud in the sky until I was invited by the
honorary officers to become principal of Jews' College and the
Chief Rabbi, Israel Brodie, vetoed my appointment.

A struggle ensued, with the honorary officers on my side and,
with only three exceptions, all of the Orthodox rabbis and ministers on the side of the Chief Rabbi. Soon after, seeing that the
Chief Rabbi was determined to veto my appointment, I resigned
as Moral Tutor at the College, a position which I had been
encouraged to occupy until the retirement of the then principal,
Dr. Epstein. When my former congregation invited me back to
be their rabbi, the Chief Rabbi refused to countenance even
this. To cut a long story short, the issue became a full blown
cause célèbre. For the first time in Anglo-Jewish history, it had
been fully spelled out that a rabbi who accepted what I have
called the nonfundamentalist view could not function as a principal of Jews' College or serve a congregation because such acceptance was incompatible with even the somewhat tepid Orthodoxy typical of Anglo-Jewry. Orthodoxy had been officially
equated with fundamentalism.

It has to be said that the debate was conducted with no holds
barred but, on the whole, without too much acrimony. It was
largely a theological question pure and simple. Since that time, I
have tried to defend my position and shall try now to repeat my
argument. My main contention has been, and is, that critical
theories regarding the origin of Jewish observances or, for that
matter, regarding the origin of the Torah itself, ought not to
render obsolete Jewish loyalty to the Torah, the Halakhah, and
the mitzvot as divine commands. The critics and the historians
have shown us how the Torah and the mitzvot came to be and
from this the picture has emerged (and it is highly plausible) of
God not only giving the Torah *to* the people of Israel but
through the people of Israel. The human element in the Torah

can no longer be denied: The Torah did not simply drop down from heaven; it has had a history. But the discovery of the history of an institution tells us nothing about the values that institution may have acquired. As thinkers of the Conservative movement in Judaism never tire of pointing out, to see it otherwise, to argue that origins can taint that which has emerged from those origins, is to commit the "genetic fallacy."

Let me try to illustrate by considering a number of Jewish rituals from the point of view of the three attitudes I have mentioned. I propose to use for these three attitudes the terms *halakhic fundamentalism* (abbreviated HF); *nonhalakhic nonfundamentalism* (NHNF); and *halakhic nonfundamentalism* (HNF).

Let us take tefillin as our first illustration. Here are the replies the holders of these three attitudes will, presumably, give in reply to the questions, Why wear tefillin? or Is it incumbent upon a religious Jew to wear tefillin?

HF: The Jew is obliged to wear tefillin because the Torah says "And thou shalt bind them for a sign upon they hand, and they shall be for frontlets between thine eyes" (Deuteronomy 6:8), and the Torah is the very word of God. We know that the verse refers to tefillin because the Rabbis inform us that this is the authentic meaning of the verse. The Rabbis know this by the tradition they received through the Oral Torah, which itself reaches back to Moses at Sinai. The same applies to all the laws governing the manufacture of the tefillin—that, for example, they have to be black and square and contain four, and no more or less than four, sections. As for the purpose of the tefillin, that is really irrelevant for practice. It is enough for us that God has His reasons. But it so happens that, in this instance, the purpose can easily be seen or, at least, one of the purposes can be seen. It is to remind the wearer of God and His Torah. True, we do not know the reason for all the details, but that belongs to the mysteries of the divine will. In short, we are obliged to wear tefillin because God has so commanded us, and, as believers in

God and His commands in the Torah, we must obey the dictates of His will.

NHNF: The verse, in all probability, as the Karaites said, and as the *Rashbam* also seems to hint,[14] can be understood figuratively; the word of God has to be with the Jew at all times as if it were bound on his hand and placed on his head. The rabbinic claim that the verse refers to tefillin is, like the doctrine of the Oral Torah upon which they base it, a rabbinic invention; perhaps the Rabbis thought prayer to be more effective if the worshiper had a concrete symbol. There is evidence that at one period, there were, in fact, five sections in the tefillin — the fifth being the Ten Commandments. There is also some evidence that when the Rabbis say that black and square tefillin are "laws given to Moses at Sinai," they mean nothing more than that the form of tefillin had been established so long before their day that it reaches back to the very beginnings of Judaism. Since, in any event, we recognize the principle of development in the Torah and acknowledge that there is a human element in it, we do not see this, or any other verse, as containing a direct divine command. It is different with regard to those ethical and religious injunctions in the Torah which can be seen as possessing permanent value. These we follow because of their value in Jewish life today. We would say that these are not true because they are in the Torah but rather that they are in the Torah because they are true. In our view, the laws regarding tefillin are manmade. An individual may choose to keep them if they have some significance to him but they are not divinely commanded. Hence it can be left to the individual. But the devout Jew who cannot see much meaning in tefillin is under no obligation to wear them.

HNF: We accept all that you say about development and the human element in the Torah. We admit that, in all probability, all the details of the tefillin and the tefillin themselves arose out of human reflection on what it is that God would have us do. Where we differ from the fundamentalist is in our recognition of the human element in the Torah, in our acknowledgement that there is no direct divine command to wear tefillin. Where we differ from the nonfundamentalist is that we cannot see why the command must be direct in order for it to be divine. After all, for whatever reason tefillin came into being among Jews, even, as may be possible, if they were talismanic or prophylactic in origin, for over two thousand years devout Jews have worn them, and that is how Jews worship God. The concrete symbol has retained its power, and that is why we do see the tefillin as God-ordained. It is this that lies behind the whole tradition of the mitzvot as commanded by God. Since it is right and proper for Jews to follow Jewish rituals in their worship of God, we can say without subterfuge: "Who has sanctified us with His commandments and commanded us to wear tefillin." Where did He command us? Through the historical experiences of the Jewish people in its long quest for the divine. Nonfundamentalists do believe that it is good to go to the synagogue to pray, even though there is no direct divine command to do so and even though scholars have succeeded in demonstrating that the institution of the synagogue has had a developing history. Furthermore, even the nonfundamentalist sees circumcision as a divine imperative, not merely an individual preference, even though no one would have thought up the rite of circumcision if it were not in the Torah. In a word, Jewish rituals belong to the collective expression by the Jewish people of its covenant with God. As such they are far more than folkways. They are commanded by God.

In connection with the dietary laws we can imagine the advocates of the three views arguing as follows:

HF: We keep all the dietary laws strictly because that is what God wishes us to do. The forbidden birds, fishes, and other animals are enumerated in Scripture. The laws against the mixing of meat and dairy dishes are derived by the Rabbis, in an authentic tradition reaching back to Moses at Sinai, from the prohibition stated in Scripture against seething a kid in its

mother's milk.[15] We do not know why the Torah chose to state
the prohibition in this way rather than to state explicitly: "Do
not cook meat and milk together," but we accept without qualification the rabbinic teaching that this is what is involved in the
prohibition. The Rabbis extended the laws so as to make a
"fence around the Torah" and we view rabbinic law as itself
sanctioned ultimately by God. We are aware that there are
debates among the codifiers regarding this or that aspect of the
dietary laws, and when we are in doubt as to which opinion is to
be followed, we consult our own rabbis. We are also aware that
Maimonides and others have suggested reasons for the dietary
laws, but, while we find these suggested reasons interesting,
these are really irrelevant to our practical religious life. Whatever
the reason or reasons, we keep the dietary laws because they are
divinely commanded. What better reason can there be? Precisely
because there is widespread neglect, nowadays, of these laws, we
tend to react by being as strict as possible, favoring this approach
over the search for leniency. If, for example, an argument is put
forward to the effect that swordfish is a permitted fish, we follow
the opinion that it is forbidden. It is admittedly not easy to keep
the dietary laws, but Judaism does make severe demands on us
and we would not have it otherwise.

NHNF: We do not believe that the dietary laws were commanded by God and instead see the various prohibitions in
Scripture as the human response to certain primitive taboos
found among many ancient peoples. We cannot know how these
arose or why the Torah chose to see particularly the taboos it did
as binding upon the people. It is probable, as Ezekiel seems to
say, that many of these laws applied originally only to the
priests,[16] and while we accept the great ideal of Israel as "a
kingdom of priests," we tend to see the ideal only in ethical and
spiritual terms. In our view, God does care whether we are coarse
or refined, whether we are good or evil; but we cannot believe
that He cares whether or not we eat lobster. Nor do we feel
ourselves bound by what the ancient Rabbis say unless we our-

selves find it to be spiritually significant. Consequently, we leave the whole question of observance of the dietary laws to the individual. Inevitably, there will be variations in practice within our ranks: Some will refrain from eating those birds, fishes, and other animals mentioned explicitly in Scripture but will have no qualms about eating meat of an animal that has not been killed by the ritual method of *shehitah*. Others will feel obligated to observe *shehitah* as well, while still others may only refrain from eating pork, the latter because of the strong abhorrence to the pig in the history of Judaism and because of the many instances when not eating pork became the test of Jewish loyalty for which Jews gave their lives. On the whole, however, most of us argue that to give too much prominence to the dietary laws is to avert attention from the really significant religious and ethical aspects of Judaism.

HNF: We agree that Scripture contains a human element, that the divine commands were, ultimately, not given in any direct fashion, and that Kashrut is important because the Jewish people in its history has decided that certain institutions have become especially sacred and binding. In this very process, however, we see the hand of God. Of course, this does not mean that we are obliged to see everything that has come down to us from the past as eternally binding by divine fiat. It all depends on how strong the attachment to a specific religious institution has been in Jewish history. What the nonfundamentalist nonhalakhist says about pork, we say of the dietary laws as a whole. Jews have lived by these laws and some have died rather than transgress them. They have become one of the main ways in which the Jewish religion finds its expression. We remain unmoved by taunts of "kitchen religion" or demands for a less corporeal approach. On the contrary, we believe that the observance of the dietary laws enhances spirituality in that it makes the observant Jew aware of the demands of religion even when he is satisfying his physical needs. As Morris Joseph once said: "Better kitchen religion than drawing room irreligion." But we differ, too, from the halakhic fundamentalist. Since, for us, God's laws are seen as mediated through the people, we are not in constant fear of transgressing a direct divine command. Consequently, although we are generally as halakhically oriented as our fundamentalist brothers and sisters, we tend towards a lenient rather than a strict interpretation of the law. We do not eat *trefa* food but will not necessarily follow every authority who decides, against other authorities, that a particular food is *trefa*.

The question of changes in the traditional liturgy has been a bone of contention among religious Jews since the experiment of the Hamburg Temple and the rabbinic opposition it provoked at the time. On this issue, the imagined debate among the upholders of the three attitudes might run as follows:

HF: We know that the Jewish liturgy is not laid down in Scripture but is post-biblical and in that sense, manmade. It was not created, however, by ordinary men but by the inspired Men of the Great Synagogue and their rabbinic successors. The laws of prayer are carefully recorded in the *Shulḥan Arukh* and are permanently binding upon all faithful Jews. We believe that the very words of the prayers contain sublime mysteries that were revealed only to those who framed the liturgy. While some of us may be prepared to countenance such minor innovations as occasional prayers in English, we reject other attempts to change the traditional prayers or even to introduce new prayers, except for the prayer for the state of Israel—which some of us oppose as well. Compared to the spiritual giants of the past, Jews today are, we believe, spiritual pygmies and dare not tamper with the liturgy, substitute the triennial for the annual Torah reading, or depart from the traditional mode of cantillation.

NFNH: Modern scholarship had succeeded in showing that the traditional liturgy has developed from the original core of the *shema* and the benedictions, and we know a great deal about the various authors of the hymns and prayers. There is, for instance, considerable discussion about the Men of the Great Synagogue, to whom the *amidah* is attributed. Discounting the suggestion by Christian scholars that the Men of the Great Synagogue were completely fictitious, it is quite obvious that the account of these as a body of 120 persons among whom were the prophets Haggai, Zechariah, and Malachi, is legendary. More likely, the liturgy was composed and put together over a long period of time by devout Jews whose formulations became acceptable to the people. Call these "inspired" if you like; we would not disagree. We see no reason, however, for supposing that all the words of the traditional liturgy are in the form of divine communications that can never be changed. While we attach great significance to the traditional liturgy and try to retain as much of it as possible, some of it contains sentiments and theological propositions to which we can no longer subscribe. Since we so not believe, for instance, that the restoration of the sacrificial system is desirable, to recite the traditional prayers longing for its return is to speak falsehood, hardly appropriate when addressing the Almighty. That is why we have felt free and, indeed, obliged to modify and change the liturgy, adapting it to our own spiritual needs.

HNF: In this area we go along with the nonhalakhic nonfundamentalists, since we, too, have adapted the traditional liturgy to reflect modern perspectives on such matters as restoration of sacrifices, for which most of us no longer pray. Where we differ is in degree: Because of our respect for the tradition, we are more resistant to change than are the nonhalakhists. We try to follow the laws as laid down in the *Shulḥan Arukh* unless such practice results in what we consider to be attitudes we can no longer entertain. We grant that there is much uncertainty here and much balancing between loyalty to the past and the need for change. In any event, it is with the idea of tradition that we operate, not with the notion of divinely inspired words which can never be changed. We do not imagine that our allegiance to the traditional forms of the liturgy can be compared with our allegiance, say, to dietary laws, if only because, as modern scholarship has shown, the liturgy itself has never been unchanging.

We might add that it is extremely unfortunate that so much
attention has been devoted to this debate, as if the main focus of
traditional Judaism was the synagogue and its services. We prefer instead to emphasize the study of the Torah as the most
significant aspect of Jewish religious life.

This leads to a further imaginary discussion by the three par-
ticipants on the question of the study of the Torah:

HF: We believe that the study of the Torah is one of the most
elevated of the mitzvot. What do we mean by the study of the
Torah? We mean the study of the very word of God as found in
the Bible and, more importantly, in the Talmud, the Midrash,
and in the works of the later authentic exponents of the Oral
Torah. We do not engage in the study as an objective exercise
but rather as an attempt to think God's thoughts after Him, so
to speak, because this is what He has commanded us to do. For
us, the Torah is contained only in the sacred books, and we
reflect on these as profoundly as we can in order to draw out
their full meaning. Our study is critical only to the extent that
we may disagree with the exposition of the Bible or the Talmud
found in this or that sacred work; if all we did was to assimilate
the ideas of our predecessors, it could not be dignified as real
study at all. It goes without saying, however, that all biblical
criticism is taboo for us. Modern critical scholarship does not
belong, for us, in the sublime category of Torah study because
this kind of scholarship tends to question the veracity of the
tradition. Nor do we seriously consider the reading of Jewish
historical works such as those by Zunz, Graetz, and Dubnow to
belong to the activity that we call the study of Torah. Some of us
may familiarize ourselves with these books and even learn from
them something about the Jewish past. But we would never
accept the view that the traditional sources should be studied
objectively. Torah study, for us, is never objective in the sense
that we can sit down before the facts unsure of where they will
lead. We know where the facts lead—to the truth as given by
God. We might, for example, when studying the book of Eccle-

siastes, take issue with some of the traditional commentators as to what the author really means. But we would never contemplate for one moment critical theories which attribute the book to other than King Solomon. Some few of us might accept critical scholarship with regard to Ecclesiastes and the other books of the Bible but would look upon this as secondary and would not generally regard it as part of Torah study. None of us would dream of even considering either Textual or the Higher Criticism of the Torah or imagine that these might contain some truth. It would be heresy for us to suggest that the ancient versions might have a better text than the Masoretic or that Moses did not write every word at the direct command of God. Precisely because we are convinced that the Torah study we engage in is sure and God ordained, we try to spend as much time as we can in this activity and our young men spend laborious years in Yeshivot without thought of a career or of any reward other than the satisfaction of "knowing Torah."

NHNF: Frankly, we find the fundamentalist attitude here quite preposterous. When all the issues have already been decided by tradition, when all the sacred texts have been removed from examination on dogmatic grounds, what remains is, we agree, a wholly admirable devotion to matters of the faith; that does not in itself, however, constitute study. We cannot possibly dismiss all the massive researches of modern scholars as heresy for to do that is to equate Judaism with obscurantism. We, too, believe in Jewish education as a supreme aim and admit that education is elevated when it receives the glorious description of Torah study. Where we differ from the fundamentalist is in our refusal to reject, on grounds of faith, all modern learning and knowledge. Since we follow the ancient Rabbis in believing that "the seal of the Holy One, blessed be He, is truth," the search for truth, wherever it is to be found, is part of what we understand as the study of the Torah. If, for example, critical scholarship has demonstrated to the satisfaction of all objective observers that the book of Ecclesiastes could not possibly have been written by King Solomon, we consider it absurd to postulate that we must continue to hold the traditional view on grounds of faith. What kind of faith is it that would have us deny the processes and conclusions of our own reasoning powers, given by God? And because of this openness, we cannot limit the study of the Torah to the study of the Talmud and the other classics of the Halakhah. For us, Jewish history, philosophy, theology, grammar and poetry are essential if a fully rounded picture of what Judaism has been—and still is—is to emerge. We admit that much of our study of the Halakhah will be a purely academic exercise since we are not bound by the traditional Halakhah in practice; many of us today, however, are freshly discovering the values inherent in the Halakhah.

HNF: Here, too, we are much closer to the nonfundamentalists than to the fundamentalists. Since we are less confident than are the fundamentalists that we have all the truth in our possession, we accept and encourage critical scholarship even when applied to the Torah. And since we like to believe that one can be objective without any sacrifice of piety, where we differ from the nonfundamentalist is in our dedication to the Halakhah as the most distinctive aspect of Judaism. For us, the study of Torah is a tremendous search for the truth through proven modern methods of investigation. And we are fortified in our quest by our belief that the search for Torah is itself Torah.

Let us now leave our imaginary debaters to look further into this idea of the quest for Torah. It is obvious that there are many problems peculiar to the nonfundamentalist approach when it is wedded to observance of the Halakhah. While, in broad outline, the view that the halakhic process is divinely guided has much to commend it, what of those halakhic rules (these are, in fact, very few in number) which seem to be unjust and at variance with the Jewish faith as a whole? To refer only to the most obvious, what of the disabilities under which women still suffer? It would be grossly unfair to accuse traditional, not to say fundamentalist,

Halakhists of indifference to human suffering but so far, for all the efforts that have been made, these problems still await solution. While in the past, nonfundamentalist Halakhists have tried to cooperate with traditionalists in trying to discover solutions that involve no departure from halakhic norms, it seems highly probable that solutions will only be found by stepping beyond these norms to interpret the Halakhah in a more liberal manner. How this is to be done is still a matter for intense debate and discussion. Part of what is involved is to try to convince outstanding Halakhists to have a less rigid view of history and thus to see Judaism as a developing religion. In other words, the nonfundamentalist Halakhist believes that knowledge of how the Halakhah has allowed extralegal considerations to influence the law in the past opens the way to an approach in which modern halakhic authorities will continue the process.

In my book *A Tree of Life* I have adduced, from the works of famous Halakhists through the ages, illustrations of how these authorities, sometimes consciously, at other times unconsciously, allowed the values of Judaism as a whole to influence their decisions.[17] While, on the surface, the Halakhists were only judges, seeking to determine what the law was, in reality they were also legislators, seeking to determine what the law should be. An examination of the history of the Halakhah reveals the operation of a kind of built-in process of development by which new conditions were allowed to effect changes in the law through the use of legal machinery: certain authorities, whose opinions had hitherto been rejected, could now be relied upon, in consideration of those new demands. Thus the Halakhah is and has always been far more flexible than it is currently made out to be when one recognizes that extralegal considerations have been introduced legally through this process — preserving both continuity and dynamism.

I have referred more than once in this lecture to the idea of a quest for the Torah, which, in essence, is where the nonfundamentalist, in his belief that all the answers have not been given, departs from the fundamentalist. For the nonfundamentalist, in many situations, it is not a question of discovering what the Halakhah has to say but rather what the Halakhah must be made to say. It might be objected that to introduce an element of uncertainty into the process is to destroy the certainty of the Halakhah. My reply is that the search for the Torah is not a newfangled invention but has respectable antecedents throughout Jewish history. What else is the whole process of Midrash if not an attempt to connect new ideas with the tradition of the past? The sixteenth-century teacher, the *Maharal* of Prague, noted that the benediction recited before studying the Torah is: "Who has sanctified us with His commandments and has commanded us to busy ourselves with words of Torah" (*laasok bedivrey Torah*). Why, asks the *Maharal*, this cumbersome expression? Why not say simply: "To study the Torah"? His reply, in so many words, is that in the process of study one cannot always be sure that one has got it right. Error is always possible in the study of any difficult subject, even more so in the attempt to discover what it is that God would have us do. Hence, the form "to busy ourselves with words of Torah." The command to study the Torah is not a demand that we actually reach the full truth, only that we be honestly engaged in seeking it. The very involvement in the quest is the essential part of the mitzvah.[18]

Such an attitude may be unsatisfying to the dogmatic mind which seeks complete certainty, but it is the only attitude that allows us to preserve our intellectual integrity. To the fundamentalist taunt that our attitude is far too vague, we can only reply that it is better to be vaguely right than definitely wrong.

> Ah, what a dusty answer gets the soul
> When hot for certainties in this our life!

We no doubt deplore with Meredith the "dustiness" of the nonfundamentalist's answers but the soul's hotness for certainties cannot always be satisfied in this life.

It would be less than honest simply to leave it at that. I must admit that once the idea of uncertainty is allowed into one's theological stance, one tends to be less scrupulous in observance of the laws. Those of us who try to keep the Halakhah as a religious imperative might still, for example, eat in a non-Jewish restaurant where, even though the food is kosher, the utensils are probably not. Although we might find some halakhic support for this practice, if we are honest we admit that we do so because the demands of the Halakhah do not really sit upon us with quite the same weight as they do for the fundamentalist, who is always apprehensive that he might be transgressing a direct divine command. What we should not do is to make our private rules into rules for everyone. In any event, even in a halakhically oriented community individuals make their own choices: Not all Orthodox married women, for example, obey the Halakhah that their heads should be covered.[19]

The well-known talmudic scholar and editor, Rabbi S.J. Sevin, once remarked that while, in the old saying, "the custom of Israel is Torah," some have inverted the phrase to imply that "the Torah of Israel is custom." Rabbi Sevin was, I imagine, criticizing the secularist's recasting of traditional Judaism into merely ethnic terms, where the mitzvot are to be kept only as folkways or as ways of preserving Jewish identity and providing the individual Jew with links to his past. It seems to me, however, summarizing the attitude I have tried to describe in this lecture, that both versions of the saying are correct. Since this view recognizes that a human element has been at work in revelation, it is ultimately the way that Jews have practiced their religion that determines what is Torah and what is not. The law in Deuteronomy that the parents of a "stubborn and rebellious son" can have him stoned to death has never been seen as a divine imperative — quite the opposite — whereas the services in the synagogue and the synagogue itself belong to the Torah because the Jewish people have considered them so. Further, the books of the Apocrypha are not part of sacred Scripture whereas the prophetic books are, because that is how the Jewish people, under divine guidance, have decided the matter. Once these "decisions" had been made, they became, on that basis alone, part of the divine Torah. The Torah of Israel may have originated in custom, but the custom became the Torah. And because there is a two way traffic in revelation — from the people to God and from God to the people — one cannot go through the Bible with a pencil and mark some passages divine and others human. The totality that we call the Torah is human imbued with the divine.

With this in mind, then, how shall we answer the vexed question, widely discussed by the medieval Halakhists: Why should rabbinic law be obeyed? It is illogical to reply that rabbinic law has biblical sanction; since it was the Rabbis who made this claim, we are thus back where we started. The only reasonable explanation is that the Rabbis were the representatives of the people and the people, accepting upon themselves the total discipline of the Torah, are the ultimate sanction for what does and does not belong to it. Thus it is utterly simplistic to argue, for instance, that the Karaites may have been right in rejecting the rabbinic tradition. What can "right" mean in this context? It cannot mean "right" in the sense of ultimate truth for that is known only to God. It may be attractive to speculate what would have been the nature of Judaism had the Karaites won out in their struggle. But that would be as pointless an exercise as trying to imagine what Judaism would be like had the Prophets spoken in Assyrian or Egyptian. The plain facts of history are that the Karaites' position was not followed and that the Prophets did speak in Hebrew. I fancy that this is what Zacharias Frankel meant when he described this approach to our religion as "positive historical Judaism": Judaism is "historical" in the sense that it has had a history and did not simply drop down ready made from heaven. And it is "positive" because that which history has shaped *is* the Jewish religion. God presumably could have revealed His will without human cooperation but He evidently did not choose to do so.

What bothers many, otherwise sympathetic to the view I have been proposing, is the prominence given to the human role. How do we know, I am frequently asked, that the Jewish people were always right in what they declared to be the Torah of God? That the question is misguided can be seen it we ask the similar question: How do we know that Hebrew is the language God wishes us to use in prayer? The obvious answer to the latter is that it is irrelevant to the prayer life of the Jew whether, as some of the medieval thinkers maintained, Hebrew was the original language of mankind. We are reminded of the old lady who began to study Hebrew in her later years so that when she went to heaven she could speak to God in his own language. On the contrary, in our view Hebrew is used in prayer only because this is the language in which the Bible was written, in which the Prophets delivered their message, and in which the prayers were largely compiled. Isaiah spoke in a different Hebrew style than Amos, both in a different style from that of Rabbi Akiba, all in a different style from that of the prayer book. Yet all used the same language albeit with a variety of nuances. Hebrew is not *lashon ha-kodesh* ("the holy tongue") because of its inherent sanctity but because of its use throughout the ages for sacred purposes. And by the same token, the Jewish religion, created though it is by the Jewish people, affords its followers, as no other religion can effectively do, with an authentic vocabulary of worship.

This brings us to the oft-discussed modern question: Is Hebrew the *only* language in which to offer Jewish prayers? While one need not be categorically opposed to changes in the Halakhah in this matter, great sensitivity is required to discern which changes can and should be introduced in the name of Judaism itself and which can only result in a distortion of the faith. That is why Frankel refused to accept the halakhic and religious reasons advanced by the early Reformers to show that

Hebrew was not essential for Jewish prayer. The individual may not be able to pray satisfactorily in Hebrew and, for him, the vernacular is acceptable. But for the Jewish community to countenance the substitution of German, French, or English for Hebrew is to do violence to the Jewish spirit. In this area *vox populi* is *vox Dei*. With no excessive license, this idea can be read into Rabbi Ishmael's dictum, "The Torah speaks in the language of men,"[20] even though Rabbi Ishmael himself did not and could not have intended his dictum to convey this meaning.

In the previous lecture I have described the view I advocated there as "liberal supernaturalism." To point to the human element in revelation is a far cry from implying that God is not the Creator of the Torah. On the contrary, it is God who makes Himself known through the human process of redaction. How this can be is a tremendous mystery, but then, so is how God can be in control of His universe and yet leave room for human freedom and human creativity. To quote the *Maharal* again, just as God created an unfinished universe for humans to bring to perfection, He created an incomplete Torah for humans to bring to completion.[21]

Three Midrashic statements with the same implications are relevant here, all derived from stories about Turnus Rufus, the Roman Governor of Palestine in the first century, and Rabbi Akiba. Turnus Rufus once asked Rabbi Akiba: Which is the greater, the work of God or the work of human beings? To his surprise, Rabbi Akiba answered: The work of human beings is greater. Why? Because God creates wheat but it is the farmer who plows the field, sows the seed, and reaps the harvest and it is the baker who makes the flour into a dough and bakes the bread for men to enjoy. This story is an advance on "God helps those who help themselves" in affirming that the human completion of God's unfinished business, so to speak, is actually greater since it is the fulfillment of the divine purpose.[22]

In another story, Turnus Rufus asks Rabbi Akiba: If God loves the poor, as you Jews say, why did He make them poor in the first instance? The Roman nobleman is suggesting here that it is positively impious to help the poor since it seems to question God's providence. If, as appears to be evident, God has made some men poor, does it not frustrate God's purpose to try to improve their lot? Rabbi Akiba replies: It is to provide the rich with the means of acquiring virtue. That is to say, God has created a world in which there is poverty as well as riches so that human beings blessed with worldly goods will learn the true purpose of human life by exercising care and compassion for the less fortunate. Far from charity being a frustration of the divine will, it is the fulfillment of the divine purpose.[23]

The third story is even more revealing of the Jewish attitude. Here Turnus Rufus asks Rabbi Akiba: If God wanted Jewish males to be circumcised, why did He create them with foreskins? Again Rabbi Akiba replies that the removal of the foreskin makes the male whole.[24]

In all three stories, the Roman is being strictly logical. You Jews, he is saying, puzzle me. On the one hand, you are always talking about the power of God and His creation of the universe, and yet you are constantly seeking to improve on His handiwork (Just as some people, in the early days of aviation, argued: If God wanted men to fly He would have given them wings). The logic is faulty in the extreme. God could have created a perfect world but then there would have remained nothing for human beings to accomplish. God has created a world in which perfection is not possible without human cooperation; George Eliot put it well: God could not create a Stradivarius violin without Stradivari. And in the third story and in the Maharal's saying the idea is applied to the Torah as well: It is not only an unfinished world that God has created but an unfinished, incomplete Torah; God cannot create the Torah of Rabbi Akiba without Rabbi Akiba; and the sign of the covenant, to have significance, requires the act of circumcision.

These three stories illustrate not only our view of *Torah min ha-shamayim* but also the difference between fundamentalist and nonfundamentalist attitudes toward Midrash. The fundamentalist, who takes all rabbinic sayings on their face value, will believe that these conversations between Turnus Rufus and Rabbi Akiba actually took place. The nonfundamentalist will not necessarily deny that they occurred, but he will appreciate that the value of the ideas they contain is not affected even if the stories are fictitious, as they probably are. The probability is that when the Jewish sages pondered the vast differences in world view between sophisticated Romans and learned Jews, they expressed their ideas in fiction just as the Prophet Nathan did when he rebuked King David by telling the story of the poor man and his ewe lamb. No one imagines that the man with the lamb really existed, just as there probably never was, as historical fact, a King Lear with three daughters. As truth about the human condition, however, Shakespeare's Lear really does exist, just as the truths inherent in biblical parable only enhance the biblical stories in which they appear.

When the fundamentalist treats fiction as fact, he fails utterly to grasp that some truths are best expressed as fiction — though it is not difficult to understand why he approaches Torah this way: Afraid that once the very notion of fiction is introduced into sacred writ or rabbinic Midrash, the very veracity of his Judaism comes into question. The halakhic nonfundamentalist, on the other hand, can view the nonfactual, nonhistorical aspects of Scripture as exclamation marks rather than question marks. This is the whole of my argument in this lecture on understanding the doctrine of *Torah min ha-shamayim* in less rigid and more human terms. If one persists in turning fiction into truth, one is in danger of turning truth into fiction.

The Concept of *ISRAEL* as Chosen
The Struggle between Particularism and Universalism; Related Eschatological Questions

IN THE PREVIOUS two lectures I have tried to describe and defend the modernist-supernaturalist approach to God and the Torah. In this lecture I shall extend that position to consider the doctrine of the Chosen People as well. Basically, there are several aspects to the concept: Did God, indeed, choose the Jewish people? And if so, how and why? The fundamentalists have no doubts about the first question and concern themselves only with speculation about the second. The naturalists have no use for either question since for them a choosing God—a Being exercising choice—does not exist. The liberal supernaturalists, on the other hand, see the whole idea of chosenness as part of the Torah, which to them is a composite of the human and the divine. Whatever meaning they attach to the doctrine, it has, they believe, been invented by the Jewish people themselves and emerged as a result of the people's reflection on the significance of their role in God's world. When it is cast in these terms, the doctrine raises the same doubts that one encounters in considering the concept of *Torah min ha-shamayim:* since a human element is acknowledged to be present, and all human effort is prone to error, the doctrine may or may not be true. With these possibilities in mind, one can also assess what permanent value there might be in perpetuating the belief that God has chosen the Jews, especially in light of the tensions such a position creates between the particularism of the Jewish religion and the

57

universalism with which we view the rest of humanity. Finally, one can consider the related eschatological doctrines which accompany the concept of Jewish peoplehood: In being chosen by God to accept the Torah, are Jews also chosen to accept certain beliefs about the coming of the Messiah, the immortality of the soul, and the resurrection of the dead?

To answer these questions, however, we must first look at the way the doctrine of the Chosen People has been understood in the Jewish tradition. We discover, on the whole, two distinct approaches which can best be described as the qualitative and the associative. Whereas in the qualitative view, being chosen means that the Jewish people has been endowed with special qualities of mind or soul, in the associative view, it simply means that the Jews, no different in essence from all other human beings, have been assigned a special role to play in the world. And while in the first view the special role given to the Jewish people is the result of their chosenness, in the second view the special role *is* their chosenness.

While, somewhat surprisingly, the Reform leader Abraham Geiger believed the Jews to be the Chosen People because they were created with a genius for religion far more highly developed than in any other people,[1] the most extreme proponents of the qualitative approach are to be found among the medieval Jewish thinkers.[2] Following the Aristotelian division of matter into minerals, plants, animals, and human beings, Judah Halevi in the *Kuzari* adds a fifth category, that of the Jewish people. Just as the difference between plants and minerals, animals and plants, human beings and animals, is not simply one of kind but also of degree, so too, the difference between Jews and other human beings is one of quality. Because Jews are descended from the righteous patriarchs, who obeyed God and with whom God made an everlasting covenant, their souls are qualitatively different from non-Jewish souls, even though their bodies are the same as other human bodies. The Jews, then, according to Halevi, constitute a spiritually superior race, and thus only the people of Israel can produce prophets. A Gentile, no matter how intelligent and moral he may be, cannot become one. His mind may be a highly gifted one, his ethical and religious conduct may be exemplary; yet he does not possess the quality of soul with which only Jews are endowed—and this he cannot attain no matter how hard he tries.

To be fair to Halevi, he is very far from suggesting that all Jews are naturally good or can do no wrong. On the contrary, precisely because they belong to a higher species, when Jews do fall they are much worse than Gentiles. Just as a dead tree is more repulsive than stagnant water, the carcass of an animal than a dead tree, and a human corpse than an animal carcass, a bad Jew is worse than any bad Gentile could possibly be. Like the little girl in the jingle, when a Jew is good he is very very good but when he is bad he is horrid.

In the Kabbalah as in the *Kuzari*, the qualitative view of chosenness predominates. In some versions, the Jewish soul is literally, "a portion of God on high"—that is to say, deep in the recesses of each Jewish psyche there is a part of the *En Sof*. Another view is that the souls of Israel come from a specially elevated place, and the perfection of the supernal realms is brought about chiefly through the acts of the body in which such souls reside and through their mental processes. A third view, in which the qualitative approach perhaps reaches its most extreme form, is to be found in Ḥabad psychology. To begin with, the divine portion of the soul is limited to Jews (and to converts to Judaism who receive this special element upon their conversion). In addition, however, the "animal souls" of Jews—which provide their basic psychic energy—derive from a spiritual force containing an admixture of good and evil, whereas the "animal souls" of Gentiles, on the other hand, derive from a different spiritual force, one that is wholly impure. The bizarre conclusion to be drawn is that Gentiles are never free from the taint of self-interest even in the good that they do.[3]

Obviously, accepting the qualitative approach to the doctrine of the Chosen People is problematic for most religious Jewish modernists, to whom all theories of racial superiority, it goes without saying, are rightly to be viewed with suspicion. Of course, in any interpretation of chosenness, the Jewish idea is totally different from any *Herrenvolk* notion, yet the danger is ever present of identifying the superior with the specially privileged. In any event, it is pointless to discuss whether the Jewish race is superior in essence since the whole notion of racial purity has been effectively exploded: Jews have mixed with other races; there have been numerous converts to Judaism; and to imagine that there are many Jewish descendants of the patriarchs with no non-Jewish blood in their veins is to court fantasy. What of the ruling, followed by Jews for well-nigh two thousand years, that the child of a Jewish mother and a Gentile father is a Jew? Furthermore, even Judah Halevi and the Kabbalists saw fit to make exceptions in order to allow the "special soul" endowment to become the entitlement of converts. Finally, who can accept the notion that Gentiles are incapable of disinterestedness? Clearly, to see the Jews as chosen because of innate qualities of mind or soul is to transform them into superhuman beings who do not really belong to the human race at all. Certainly in some versions of this approach the Jews appear as alien visitors to the planet, arriving, as in science fiction, to instruct the benighted inhabitants on how to conduct their affairs.

The associative view, in which Jews are only assigned a special role to play, is far more palatable. In this approach, Jews are singled out only to fulfill the commandments as divinely ordered through acceptance of the Torah, and the very fact that the descendants of the patriarchs have held fast to this covenant made with their ancestors makes for chosenness. Thus the benediction recited before the reading of the Torah should not be translated "who has chosen us from all peoples and has given us His Torah" but "who has chosen us from all peoples *by* giving us His Torah." As Saadiah Gaon put it, "Our people is only a people by virtue of the Torah."[4] There is even a talmudic saying to the effect that Jews are by nature an intolerable people to whom the Torah had to be given in order to tame their guile and ferocity.[5]

Even this comparatively mild interpretation of the doctrine of chosenness, however, generates a considerable amount of tension between the particular and the universalistic — between belief in the God who chose the Jews and belief in the God of all humanity. On the one hand, Judaism centers around a people, without whom there can be no Jewish religion. On the other hand, however, the God Jews worship is the God of all the earth: the well-being of all humans is His concern. He is thus the God of the Jews but most emphatically, He is *not* a Jewish God. When Jews rightly stress the universalistic aspects of their religion, they are doing something far greater than expressing their tolerance or engaging in apologetics. They are seeking to understand the essence of the Almighty. If He is thought of as being interested solely in the physical and spiritual well-being of His own people (some Jews, unfortunately, have entertained such a grotesque notion), the thought in the mind is something other than God.

A classical summary of the traditional Jewish position in this matter is attributed, in *Ethics of the Fathers*, to Rabbi Akiba: "Beloved is man for he is created in the image of God. Beloved are the people of Israel for they are called the children of God."[6] There is bound to be an element of triumphalism in a religion that considers itself to be true. There is something special about Judaism, something which makes it uniquely different from any other religion. But triumphalism must never be so stretched as to exclude other men from God's loving care, any more than universalism should be stretched so as to weaken or destroy that which makes Judaism unique. Rabbi Akiba, in the saying attributed to him, expresses the proper universalistic attitude by affirming that every human being is created in God's image. And he expresses the special relationship between God and the Jewish people by comparing it to the relationship of father to child. On the whole, however, and despite Jewish apologetics, Judaism does not use the expression "the fatherhood of God" to denote that all men are His children.[7] The special relationship denoted by "father" is usually reserved for that between God and the people of Israel. Consequently, the expression "the fatherhood of God and the brotherhood of man" is also untypical. That all men are, in a sense, brothers or, at least, cousins, is implied in the table of nations in Genesis where all human beings belong to the various branches of Noah's family.[8] But the brotherhood of man is not derived from the idea of the fatherhood of God—and there is no cause for embarrassment in this: The Jewish people, by wishing to have a special relationship with God and by striving always to be true to that relationship, adopt it with pride as the badge not of their uniqueness but of the uniqueness of their religion.

Having said this I must point to a remarkable, even if unhistorical, comment by Rabbi Meir Simhah Kahan of Dvinsk in Latvia in his commentary to the Torah entitled *Meshekh Ḥokhmah.*[9] Rabbi Kahan notes that in the book of Exodus, Israel is described as God's firstborn. What is special about a firstborn? It is he or she that gives the father and mother their names. The parents love all their children, yet the firstborn is the one that made them into parents. God loves all His children; He is the Father of all mankind. But it was the people of Israel who first discovered God and hailed Him as Father.

Perhaps it is relevant at this point to consider the Noachide Laws. Although the Torah in its fullness was given to Israel alone, the Rabbis developed the idea of a Torah for the Gentiles known as the seven precepts of the sons of Noah, so-called because Noah was the father of the human race after the Deluge; the Rabbis, however, actually trace the seven precepts back to the real father of the human race, Adam.

If we revert for a few moments to the theme of the second lecture, the fundamentalist will accept the existence of these laws literally. The Rabbis did not "develop" the seven precepts: they merely recorded the tradition, going back to Moses at Sinai, that God gave them to Adam. Noah, Adam's descendant, obeyed them and passed them on his sons and through them to the entire human race. In the nonfundamentalist view, it is doubtful whether Noah is an historical figure, and the story of Adam and Eve is mythological, which is not to say that it has no value. Truth is often conveyed through stories, as we have noted. In this view, what the Rabbis were doing, over a fairly long period, was to reflect on the meaning of the Torah for the non-Jewish world. Convinced that God has designs for all His creatures, the Rabbis asked themselves: Granted that the full observance of the Torah is for the Jewish people alone, what are the basic rules by which all human beings are expected to live? Grotius saw this clearly when he used this very rabbinic doctrine to develop his idea of natural law—that is, a series of basic rules to which all human beings can give their assent because of their basic human nature. According to the nonfundamentalist, then, this is the background of the Noachide Laws, which are attributed to Noah and to Adam, the fathers of the human race. As stated in the Talmud[10] (after debates on some of the details) they are: 1) the prohibition of idolatry; 2) the prohibition of adultery and incest; 3) the prohibition of murder; 4) the prohibition of eating a limb torn from a living animal; 5) the prohibition of blasphemy; 6) the prohibition of theft; 7) that there must be an adequate system of justice and law enforcement. In the language of our day, then, the Torah makes comparatively few demands on non-Jews; it does, however, require that they create a just society with proper respect for human life and property, proper concern for animal life, and reverence for God. Gentiles who keep the seven Noachide Laws are referred to as "the saints of the nations of the world," and they have "a share in the world to come"—that is, they are assured of "salvation." Actually, the term "the saints of the nations of the world" is late. The original term is "the righteous of the nation of the world."[11] Gentiles do not have to be saints but ordinary good men and women in order to merit salvation.

Admittedly, a good deal of this is purely theoretical. It is unlikely in the extreme that Gentiles ever asked Rabbis which rules they are expected to obey. The chief concern here is with Jewish attitudes towards non-Jews. It has often been pointed out that in times of religious persecution, Jewish attitudes towards Gentiles hardened and became increasingly exclusive, while in times of comparative security and tranquillity, the tendency was in the direction of greater acceptance of the worth of the outside world. Thus in rabbinic times, there were often very adverse judgments about "the pagan idolaters" whereas later a marked tendency to treat Moslems and Christians as belonging to "the righteous of the nations of the world" can be observed.

For a number of reasons, the problem of universalism versus particularism in Judaism has become more complicated in the modern world. First, there has emerged the idea, inconceivable in the Middle Ages, of religious tolerance and the right of every human being to practice freely his or her own religion or to practice none. This relaxation of rigidity does not necessarily result in the weakening of modern faith. While most of us today admit that not everything of value in human life is contained in the Jewish tradition, there is no need for this to result in relativism or the attitude that religion is not really important. We still can and should hold fast to the truths that have been given to our ancestors but without too much of their exclusiveness: We are less inclined, for instance, to deny the title "the righteous of the nations of the world" to the adherents of other religions or to atheists if they lead decent lives, for we tend to see ethical conduct as cutting across the religious barriers of mankind. And while the idea of religious tolerance is certainly new, such an attitude is not entirely without support in the tradition. There is Rabbi Akiba's dictum, for example, that all human beings are created in God's image or the rabbinic teaching that a child brought up among idolaters is not to be blamed for the pagan rites he observes when he grows up.[12]

It seems to me that we can go even further, however, if we take seriously the idea of divine providence. Since God allowed the polytheistic religions to develop—and atheism, too, for that matter—can it not be said that, while the devout Jew must certainly reject these alien philosophies, it is not for him to condemn those who hold to them since, for all we know to the contrary, this might be the way in which God speaks to the Hindu, the Buddhist, the primitive animist, the agnostic, and the atheist? In any event, these

matters can safely be left to God, under whose judgment we all
live. For practical purposes, however, Jews can, and on the whole,
do behave in brotherly fashion towards all other decent human
beings. It is ironic that the majority of Jews are tolerant and friendly
to non-Jews of whatever persuasion (except, of course, to antisemites) but are far less inclined to be tolerant of fellow Jews whose
religious philosophies differ from their own. This leads to the further complications that have come about through the rise of secular
Zionism and the establishment of the state of Israel.

In the traditional picture sketched above, a division has always
existed between the Jewish people, on the one hand, and the
"nations of the world" or "the Noachides" on the other. In terms of
modern political geography, however, we speak today not of "the
nations" but rather of individual nation-states, of which the Jews
may or may not be considered as one. With the establishment of
the state of Israel, the Jewish people have become a nation in the
secular sense while Jews in the Diaspora generally continue in the
tradition of peoplehood, the latter mostly conceived of in religious
terms. The struggle between the religious and the secularists within
the state of Israel, then, concerns not only practices and observances, but, more fundamentally, whether Jewish peoplehood is to
be defined in national or religious terms. Most Jews today are
totally committed to the well-being of the state of Israel, but that
does not mean that they are bound to accept the nationalistic
ideology. Nor are all Jews living in Israel willing to accept a religious
ideology totally based on the Torah and rabbinic law.

That these two attitudes do not easily coexist is sadly evident in
the fierce "Who is a Jew?" debate which has recently erupted with a
vehemence on both sides that overlooks the obvious—that the
debate concerns only the "secular" definition of the Law of Return
and has little or nothing to do with the very different question of
how the doctrine of Jewish peoplehood, conceived of in religious
terms, can be interpreted so as to embrace the secularists. In reality,
the Jewish tradition itself has, on the whole, an attitude of nonex-
clusiveness. After all, the Talmud speaks of "the sinners in Israel"

being as full of mitzvot as the pomegranate is full of seeds (*Hagigah* 27a); of "whoever denies idolatry is called a Jew" (*Megillah* 13a); and of "a fast-day in which sinners do not participate is no fast-day" (*Keritot* 6b). To be sure, this does not touch on the more complicated questions dealing with those Jews who have rejected all basic religious belief. It is true, for example, that there is no ruling anywhere in the classical sources that a Jewish atheist cannot help to make up the minyan, the quorum for public worship. But that, Solomon Schechter has rightly said, is because such a bizarre notion as a Jewish atheist attending the synagogue for prayer was beyond the imagination of the Jewish teachers.[13] Generally speaking, however, no tests of belief are applied to applicants for synagogue membership. It is assumed that the desire to join the worshipers and participate in the service is evidence enough that, albeit in a very vague manner, the applicant assents to the basic beliefs. In fact, the test of belief in its most ruthless form was only applied by Maimonides, obedient to his own atypical view that Jewish peoplehood is to be defined in terms of dogmas:

> When all these principles are in the safe keeping of man, and his conviction of them is well established, he then enters into the general body of Israel, and it is incumbent upon us to love him, to care for him, and to do for him all that God commanded us to do for one another in the way of affection and brotherly sympathy. And this, even though he were guilty of every possible transgression, by reason of the power of desire or the mastery of the base material passions. He will receive punishment according to the measure of his perversity, but he will have a portion in the world to come, even though he be of the transgressors in Israel. When, however, a man breaks away from any of these fundamental principles of belief, then of him it is said that he has left the general body of Israel and he denies the root of Judaism. And he is termed *min* [heretic] and *epikorus* [unbeliever] and it is obligatory upon us to hate him and cause him to perish, and it is concerning him that the scriptural verse says "Shall I not hate those who hate Thee, O Lord?" [Ps. 139:21][14]

Even the most rabid fundamentalist would not subscribe to such medievalism nowadays. Indeed, to their credit, a number of modern Orthodox thinkers have expounded a view of the doctrine of Jewish unity that would virtually exclude only those Jews who themselves do not wish to be included—by embracing another religion, for instance.[15] And while it is no use pretending that Jewish ecumenism is alive and completely well today, the Holocaust and the establishment of the state of Israel have both drawn Jews together in a way unimagined in the first decade of this century. Thus there is a kind of guarded consensus among religious Jews—whether Orthodox, Reform, or Conservative—to see whatever divine role that exists for the Jewish people as applying to the people as a whole: "Thou art One, and Thy name is One, and who is like unto Thy people Israel, One nation upon earth?"

The emphasis in Judaism on the Chosen People idea, however, creates tensions in another area as well: What of the individual Jew or, for that matter, the individual non-Jew? What is the divine plan for each individual in his or her own right, not simply as members of the group? The group is, in fact, no weightier than the individuals of which it is comprised, so that while it is true that the individual only finds complete fulfillment within the group, it is the group that exists for its individual members and not, as in totalitarian systems, the other way around.

From the religious point of view, Jewish peoplehood stands midway between universalism on the one hand and the individual soul hungry for God on the other. As we have noted, Jewish thinkers have diverse views on the relationship of these two components. The talmudic rabbis—naturally so in view of the threat to Jewish peoplehood in their day—tended to place much of the emphasis on the group. The need for a minyan for prayer, of course, is the prime example. In addition, most of the statutory prayers are supplications for the Jewish people as a whole rather than personal invocations to God. Maimonides, on the other hand, felt that the community exists primarily to promote suitable conditions in which the individual can be free to worship.[16] This is not to say, of course, that he was unaware of the strong claims society has on every Jew, just as the Rabbis certainly did not fail to consider the high worth of every individual.

Nowhere in the rabbinic literature is that worth stressed more emphatically than in the Mishnah tractate *Sanhedrin*, which deals with witnesses in a capital charge who are about to testify that a man has committed a murder.[17] The witnesses must be warned, says the Mishnah, of the seriousness of their offense if the man against whom they are about to testify is really innocent of the charge. They are to be told that Adam was created as a single individual and that this teaches us "whoever destroys a single human life it is as if he had destroyed a whole world and whoever saves a single human life it is as if he had saved the whole world." The Mishnah adds other reasons why Adam was created as a single individual. It is to teach that no man can say to any other: My ancestors were greater than yours (since all are descended from the same couple, Adam and Eve). Further, it teaches the greatness of the Almighty who created all mankind from the same couple, and yet created no two individuals exactly alike, no two completely identical in form, features and temperament. Finally, it teaches that there is only one Creator, not a series of creators, each bringing his own favorites into being.

The meaning is obvious (and it might be necessary to repeat that in the nonfundamentalist view the lesson is also abundantly clear; even if Adam and Eve are only mythological figures the lesson is still cogent as ever): One God created all human beings, endowing each with individual significance, each with unique features, each created in the image of God, and all created as equals. Each individual is a whole world in himself. Moreover, it is clear from the context (especially the proof from Adam) that the reference is to every individual, whether Jew or non-Jew. Unfortunately, somewhere along the line, a narrow-minded copyist inserted the words "of Israel" so that the text now reads,

"Whoever destroys a single life of Israel [that is, a single *Jewish* life], it is as if he had destroyed a whole world and, whoever saves a single Jewish life, it is as if he had saved a whole world." But apart from the question of context, none of the ancient versions add "of Israel," and thus the statement is truly universalistic with its application to every individual, whether Jewish or non-Jewish.[18]

There are thus severe tensions with which we have to live and which we can respond to creatively, if we are so minded, between the universalistic thrust of Judaism and the particularistic; between the acknowledgment of Judaism as the true religion and the recognition that there is truth in other religions; between the understanding of Judaism both in nationalistic and in religious terms, and resulting from this latter, between the need to affirm the religious stance and yet cooperate with the secularists in helping to promote the welfare of the state of Israel and of Jews everywhere.

But acceptance of the doctrine of the Chosen People brings with it other ideological considerations. Reference has been made to the "world to come." Here is the place to consider the whole question of Jewish eschatology, of the last days, beliefs not about that which has happened in the past but about what will happen in the future. Before we can determine whether they can be accepted or rejected from the position of liberal supernaturalism, however, we must first describe briefly the traditional ways these doctrines have been viewed (although even in this area much is purely speculative).

In the tradition, the term "the world to come" means either the new world of the resurrection of the dead or the world of souls—that is to say, "heaven," though neither this term nor the term "paradise" is normally used for this state in the Jewish tradition. A related doctrine has to do with the coming of the Messiah in this world. What we have here, from the historical point of view, is an amalgam of various eschatological ideas, the formulation of which probably took place during the early rabbinic period—around the beginning of the present era.

The broad picture which emerges is as follows: When a man dies, his soul survives the death of his body and enters into the world of spirits. There it is judged for its deeds on earth. If it was righteous, it is deemed worthy to enter heaven (*Gan Eden*) to enjoy the bliss of nearness to God—or in the language of the Rabbis, to bask in the radiance of the Shekhinah.[19] If the soul was wicked, however, it is to be condemned to suffer for its sins in *Gehinnom* (hell) for a twelve month period before being allowed into *Gan Eden*. The soul of an average man—neither completely righteous nor completely wicked—is to be condemned to *Gehinnom* for a lesser period.

Meanwhile, according to the tradition, human history is moving continually toward fulfillment of the "world to come." At a time set aside by God (or earlier, if mankind is worthy), God will send His Messiah, a descendant of the House of David, who will lead the Jewish people back to the Holy Land. The Temple will be rebuilt and the sacrificial system reintroduced. In this period, the Jewish people will be completely free from persecution and eventually all men will acknowledge God as King over all. War will be abolished, and all men will live in harmony and peace. Some time after the advent of the Messiah, the bodies of all the dead will be resurrected and united with their souls. There will then be a further great Day of Judgment, and those considered worthy will live forever on earth in a purely spiritual state where no eating, drinking, or other physical pursuits will be necessary, since the flesh of the righteous will be composed of a specially refined substance. Needless to say, such a state is completely unimaginable for us in our coarse bodies: All we can understand is that the reward of the righteous will be to enjoy the pleasure of the nearness of God for all eternity—the degree and intensity of that pleasure to depend on the deeds performed during a person's lifetime on earth.

Presented in this way, the entire eschatological scheme is incredibly crude, a far too tidy picture of what is, on any showing, a tremendous mystery. More accurately, as even the Jewish teachers of the past acknowledged, the traditional view is only a shorthand description of that which is basically indescribable, only the barest outlines of which have been crystallized into dogma, the details having been left to God. Even such a dogmatic thinker as Maimonides, expounder of the Thirteen Principles of the Faith, was virtually silent on the question of the resurrection of the dead for most of his life. Accused of denying the doctrine entirely, he finally wrote his "Essay on the Resurrection," in which he qualifies his views: The resurrected dead will, indeed, live on earth for a very long period; ultimately, however, their bodies will return to dust and their souls alone will be immortal. Further, Maimonides ridicules those messianic folk-beliefs that predict wondrous miracles at the end of days: loaves of bread, for example, appearing suddenly on trees. All such notions, he boldly remarks, even if found in the talmudic/midrashic literature, belong only to pure speculation and not to Jewish dogma. Although he does believe in a personal messiah under whose guidance the Temple will be rebuilt and the sacrificial system restored in its entirety, Maimonides is ambiguous on the question of *Gehinnom*, which he identifies not with actual torment but with the annihilation of the souls of the very worst sinners. The vast controversy which erupted after Maimonides' death, then, was partly a result of the great sage's views on eschatology.[20]

Other, less refined views, were held in the Middle Ages in the antiphilosophical schools of the time. One prevalent idea was that the third Temple will not be built by human hands but will drop down intact from heaven. Another was that *Gehinnom* is an actual place of torture, albeit, the more sophisticated suggested, of spiritual torment, the anguish suffered by the soul remote from God. Again, in these schools, it was believed that the resurrected dead will live forever on earth, albeit, as

Nahmanides observed, in a subtly refined body.[21] And some of the antiphilosophical teachers went so far as to take literally the statements in the rabbinic literature that, in the hereafter, God will arrange a great banquet for the righteous in which King David will take the cup of wine and recite the Grace after Meals. For Maimonides, since there are no bodies and only souls in "the world to come," such statements refer only to spiritual delights. For example, when the Rabbis say that the righteous will sit with their crowns on their heads and bask in the radiance of the Shekhinah, this cannot be taken literally. The Maimonidean interpretation of the "sitting" in this context refers not to any physical reality but rather to the tranquil spiritual state of the souls of the righteous. And the "crowns" are reflections of the truth and knowledge about God which they attain through their deeds while on earth.[22]

With the rise of modern rationalism, the tendency among Jewish theologians has been to further downplay the miraculous and marvelous element in the traditional eschatological scheme. Reform thinkers in Germany in the nineteenth century, and later in the United States, gave up the idea of a personal messiah in favor of the concept of a Messianic Age which would come about not by a miraculous divine intervention but by the gradual progress of humanity towards the establishment of a just society with better educational prospects available to all. Moreover, Western Civilization was itself seen as heralding the Messianic Age. Before the rise of antisemitism, before two global wars of catastrophic dimension, before the Holocaust and the gas-chambers, before Hiroshima and Nagasaki, before the Stalinist purges, it was by no means a case of wishful thinking to believe the Western world was moving speedily towards the millennium. It is tragic that the dream has been shattered, but it is wrong to scorn those who once kept it alive, believing it to be a legitimate spelling out of the messianic dogma.

Zionism has provided another version of the messianic idea, a secular version, to be sure, but also based on the age-old doc-

trine. Jews, the Zionists affirmed, would realize the messianic
dream if they had the will to do so—in Herzl's words, "If you
wish it, it is no dream." In our day, the dream has been realized:
the state of Israel has been a living reality for over forty years.
Zionism, however, is a secular philosophy, with little of the
numinous quality of the original belief in the Messiah. This is
why some religious Jews, while accepting that the emergence
and continued success of the state of Israel are providential, still
refuse to see it in messianic terms. Others have tried to have it
both ways. The state of Israel is not actually to be identified with
the Messianic Age per se. The Messiah has still to come, but the
state of Israel is "the beginning of the Redemption"—*athalta
de-geulah,* a concept for which there is little support in the
tradition. Either the Messiah has come or he has not come. There
is no middle ground in which he has only partly arrived.

Thus we moderns are presented with a wide range of concepts
upon which to base our own views of "the world to come." While
most secular Jews reject the whole eschatological scheme,
whether in its traditional or modernist interpretation, the Jewish
fundamentalist will accept all of the doctrines of the "last
days"—the coming of the personal messiah, the immortality of
the soul, the resurrection of the dead—as divinely communicated truth, though he will probably admit that some of the
details remain vague and speculative. He might quote, for
example, Maimonides' statement that to seek to grasp the nature
of pure spiritual bliss in the hereafter is as impossible as for a
man born blind to grasp the nature of color.[23] If one were to ask
the fundamentalist how he knows the scheme is true, he would
justifiably reply that it is all clearly mapped out in the rabbinic
literature and this, as part of the Torah, has a built-in guarantee
against error. The nonfundamentalist cannot leave it simply at
that since, for him, the Torah has a human element. This means
that, for him, it is not only the various details that are the result
of human speculation—on this the fundamentalist will probably
agree—but the whole scheme. The nonfundamentalist, commit-

ted though he is to Judaism, will accept those parts of the
scheme which cohere with his thought and experience. He will
not ask simply what the tradition says but rather what is behind
the traditional formulations, what were the motivations for
devout Jews so reflecting on the meaning of Judaism that they
came up, over a long period, with these eschatological doctrines.
In other words, he will ask, as he does of the Torah as a whole,
which aspects of the doctrine "make sense" in light of modern
knowledge and which no longer "make sense"; which are eternal
and which time-bound; which are so much part of the Jewish
religion that their rejection involves a complete distortion of the
faith and which can safely be left to speculation or subject to
revision. Put in this way, there is bound to be a subtle balancing
of opinions, especially in this area where knock-down proof is
obviously not to be attained.

Pursuing this line of argument, I would maintain that the
only course to be adopted is one of reverent agnosticism with
regard to such doctrines as that of the Messiah and the resurrection of the dead. To me, these are philosophical rather than
religious issues, and while it seems highly unlikely that God will
eventually send a person to redeem His people and all mankind,
we cannot state categorically that this will not occur. To be honest, my faith in God is not affected if I doubt whether the
Messiah will really come one day or whether the dead will one
day be revived. These belong to the working of God's plans for
mankind and one can and should leave all this to Him. The
doctrine of the immortality of the soul, however, is an entirely
different matter. If death is the end, if there is no after-life, if
God has created only to destroy, I cannot reconcile these realities
with the God as taught by Judaism.

There seems to be, in fact, something of a contradiction
between the doctrine of the Messiah or the Messianic Age and
the doctrine of the immortality of the soul. If the true aim of
human life is to prepare the soul so that it may eventually enjoy
the bliss of the nearness of God for all eternity, if this world is, in

Keats's famous phrase, "a vale of soul-making," then why does the Messiah need to come at all and establish God's Kingdom on earth? Maimonides, dealing with this kind of question, replied that in the Messianic Age it will be easier for men to worship God in tranquillity and hence equip themselves for eternal bliss in the hereafter.[24] Such a view is not entirely implausible, but since countless human beings have, presumably, managed to engage in "soul-making" despite, or even because of, the hindrances in the pre-Messianic Age, why should there be this special period in which it is "easier" to achieve the desired end? Can it not be argued that the struggle itself contributes to the "soul-making," that a better soul is "made," so to speak, when tried in the fires of adversity?

Speculative though it is, perhaps the tradition is telling us that human life should be lived on two levels, the this-worldly and the other-worldly. Perhaps we ought to live as if this world were all so that the culmination of human history, if God's justice is to be vindicated on earth, can only occur in the Messianic Age. And yet, on a different level, we ought to live as if the sole purpose of life is to equip ourselves to enjoy the nearness of God in the hereafter. Seen in this way, the answer to the question of whether Judaism is a this-worldly or an other-worldly religion is that it is both. In *Ethics of the Fathers*, a second-century teacher remarks: "Better is one hour of spiritual bliss in the world to come than the whole of this world and yet better is one hour of repentance and good deeds in this world than the whole of the world to come."[25] This is a paradox but a profound paradox: "The world to come" is truly another world, totally different from the world of our experience and can only be in the background of our thoughts as an affirmation, in faith, that God will not allow the souls of any of His creatures to suffer the final destruction. Meanwhile, since God has placed us here, our task is to work for the "salvation" of Israel and mankind on earth and in the process to acquire our souls. It is told of a Yeshiva student at the Mir Yeshivah in Lithuania that he spent a half-hour, as the members of the Musar school are wont to do, chanting the opening words of Moshe Hayyim Luzzatto's *The Path of the Upright*: the aim of human life, this work states, is for man to enjoy the nearness of God in the next world; there is no greater delight. At the end of the half-hour the devout student closed the book firmly and said, "All very true, yet this world is also a world."

Keats's "soul-making" concept is further reflected in Jewish thought in Luzzatto's notion of "bread of shame." A poor man, says Luzzatto, will be more content to eat the morsel he has earned with the sweat of his brow than to enjoy the greatest delicacies at the table of a rich man who invited him out of charity. In the latter case, the food is bitter, the "bread of shame."[26] God has created man with a stern sense of independence: even precious divinely given spiritual gifts have to be earned. In order to be God-like, man must make the good his own—hence his probationary period on earth in which, confronted with both good and evil, he freely chooses the good. Thus, it is superficial to see the hereafter in tit-for-tat terms, God "rewarding" man in heaven for his deeds on earth. It is rather that by doing good on earth man makes the good his own for all eternity.

In the same vein, it would be sheer sentimentalism to reject entirely the notion of *Gehinnom*. If the whole purpose of the probationary period on earth is for man to acquire goodness by freely choosing it, surely the man who chooses evil must free himself from that self-acquired evil by a remorse that undoes it. In this view, which makes sense to me, heaven and hell are not places of reward and punishment, though they are often described that way. Instead, they are states of the soul. In the well-known Hasidic tale, when a Hasid wishes to observe the paradise of the Tannaim, he is shown a bare room with a Tanna sitting at a table. "Is that all?" the Hasid asks. "Yes," he is told. "The Tanna is not in paradise. Paradise is in the Tanna."

Venturing into the realm of speculation, one may consider the idea put forward by the mystics that eternity is not simply endless duration in time but outside time altogether—an Eternal Now in which past, present and future are combined. A further elaboration, again purely speculative, is that all souls become, at the death of the body, part of the Mind of God, so to speak, while retaining their individual identities.[27]

However the immortality of the soul is understood, the essential aspect is that God does not create only eventually to destroy. If, at the end, all human souls vanish into the nothingness from whence they came, what is the purpose of creation? The "experiment" is a failure from the start. This is often countered, nowadays, by saying that a man lives on in his work and in the hearts and minds made better by his existence. But this is mere sleight of hand. It is not Shakespeare who lives on in his works; it is the works that live on. And, since the whole solar system is moving to its ultimate destruction, as we are told by the scientists, the time will come when the works themselves will be no more. Needless to say, this approach provides little satisfaction to the soul longing for immortality.

In the first lecture, I tried to explore the meaning of a personal God. Here I would extend that meaning to denote the Being who guarantees the survival in some form of the individual soul. While the survival of the soul is theoretically and philosophically possible if God is understood as the impersonal power that makes for righteousness (some atheists believe in immortality), that survival can only be *guaranteed* by the God who is Himself a person or, as we have suggested as a better formulation, not less than a person. The religious reason for believing in survival is the one that follows from a belief in God. Kant saw this when he argued that God and immortality are both required by the practical reason, though not by the theoretical reason.

If one does not believe in God, one must make the most of life as it is and try to live worthily even though death comes to all at the end. To the religious mind, this is surely a bleak philosophy and one contrary to the deepest strivings of the human person: Most of us want to live forever. To call this wishful thinking is only acceptable if, in reality, God does not exist and we wish ourselves into belief in His existence in order to "guarantee" our immortality. For the believer, the wish to survive is present because God does exist and He has placed the desire for survival in our hearts. This is the religious soul's yearning, which some scorn as a selfish refusal to do good unless one is rewarded in the hereafter. Here again, however, much depends on the motivation. The truly religious person, who in brief moments attains glimpses of delight when worshiping the Almighty, is on a high plane of religious existence when he longs for the state when he will never be separated from his maker. This longing is no more selfish or unworthy than is the desire of a lover to be united with his beloved. As C.S. Lewis has put it, it is safe to assure the pure in heart that they will see God because only the pure in heart wish to do so. Needless to say, this does not mean that the religious soul longs for the death of the body. Especially in Judaism, this world has its own value, and it is here that God has placed us to lead the good life. That is why the rabbinic tradition describes this life as the place of effort and the next world as the place of reward. It is cowardly to wish to have the bliss without the effort, which is why suicide is so strongly frowned upon in Judaism. But the whole quality of life on earth is enhanced immeasurably when seen as of immense significance not only in itself but as preparation for eternity.[28]

Perhaps the strongest objection to belief in the survival of the soul after the death of the body is the obvious relationship of the mind or soul with the body. When the brain is damaged, for instance, the mind ceases to function properly and, presumably, when the brain dies there are no mental processes at all. There is no evidence, however, for identifying the brain with the soul, except as a temporary vessel to be used only until the soul enters eternity — at which time the poor instrument can be discarded. A space traveler, while in space, cannot survive without his space suit, but once he returns to earth he can breathe freely without it. And in Ewing's illustration, it does not follow from the fact that in the house I can only see the sky through the window that I cannot see the sky without the window when I leave the house.[29]

Precisely because there is a balance in Judaism between this-worldly and other-worldly concerns, the emphasis should be on the former since that is where we are in the here and now; this is where God has placed us. There are numerous tales of saintly Jewish men and women weeping on their deathbeds. They believe in perfect faith that they are about to depart for the world of truth and perfect bliss. The place of struggle for the good, however, has its own value, and while the other world is, no doubt, an inestimably more delightful mode of existence, it is still a venture into the unknown and the end of a struggle worthwhile in itself. The fifteenth-century Jewish philosopher Joseph Albo remarked that people weep at the thought of death for the same reason that a newly born child weeps when it emerges from its mother's womb. There it was secure and now a new world is opening up for it.[30] In faith we believe, indeed, in the security of the next world even as we are fully aware of the insecurities of this world. Yet this is our world, the only one we know by experience, and to leave it to become pure spirit is bound to be frightening.

That I have given so much prominence to the doctrine of the soul's immortality in a lecture on Jewish peoplehood might seem odd or even grotesque. My excuse, if such is required, is that without a belief in immortality, Judaism is not only impoverished but suffers a complete transformation. At least from early rabbinic times, faithful Jews have believed that the soul is immortal, not as an optional belief added to the religion but as the very essence of it. I do not deny for one moment that Judaism can exist without any belief in immortality, just as in one form of Buddhism, there is no belief in God. The question is whether such a radical reinterpretation — in which both the doctrines of a personal God and the immortality of the individual soul are rejected—can still qualify as traditional Judaism. Equally important, can a completely this-worldly, naturalistic faith really satisfy the religious mind and soul in quest of God? In Kolakowski's powerful words:

> If personal life is doomed to irreversible destruction, so are all the fruits of human creativity, whether material or spiritual, and it does not matter how long we, or our performances, might last. There is little difference between the works of Giovanni Papini's imaginary sculptor carving his statues in smoke for a few seconds duration, and Michaelangelo's "immortal" marbles. And even if we do imagine that there is somewhere a god who turns the wheel of life, His presence is utterly indifferent to us: He may find an incomprehensible amusement in running and watching our destiny but in a while He will throw away the universe as a broken toy. . . .This is indeed the spontaneous reaction of a believer: if nothing remains of human effort, if only God is real, and the world, after meeting its final fate, leaves its creator to the same void or plenitude He has always enjoyed, then truly it does not matter whether this hidden King exists at all. The point of this response is not that we selfishly crave a celestial reward or an infinite compensation for our finite misery, as the critics of religion have argued, but that if nothing endures save God, even God grows no better or richer as a result of human toil and suffering, and an endless emptiness is the last word of Being. If the course of the universe and of human affairs has no meaning related to eternity, it has no meaning at all.[31]

Summary

MY CONTENTION in these three lectures has been that the attitude I have called liberal supernaturalism, the attitude that is adopted, I would maintain, by very many contemporary Jews, does justice both to the Jewish tradition and to modern thought in a way rival philosophies of Judaism do not. I have argued that fundamentalism, strong on supernaturalism, either ignores or is hostile to modern scholarship, while religious naturalism, strong in its acceptance of scholarship, is weak in its understanding of God and the hereafter. Those of us who hold to liberal supernaturalism differ from the fundamentalists only in degree, our attitudes towards revelation being more open and more intellectually cogent. But our differences with religious naturalism are not only of degree but of kind. The differences are about the essential nature of Judaism as a religion.

Let us set side by side the two philosophies of Judaism — the naturalistic and the supernaturalistic. In the naturalistic view, God is not a Being or a person but an impersonal force of great significance that makes for righteousness. It would be gratuitous to argue that such a God cannot be worshiped. After all, religious naturalists do pray in synagogues and are evidently sincere. But such a God cannot reveal His will to us through the Torah since "He" has no will. Nor can such a God guarantee the immortality of the individual soul. Indeed, the whole area of eschatological belief is either totally ignored by the naturalists or, at best, radically interpreted in terms of the physical and spiritual betterment of human life in the here and now.

For us, the liberal supernaturalists, God is more than a person but not less. We find it impossible to understand how the human mind can have emerged unless there is Mind behind and beyond the universe. And we believe that our highest strivings are not doomed to ultimate extinction but that we live on for all eternity

with God who brought us into being. We believe, too, that God
has not left us without guidance and that the Torah is God's blue-
print for the universe, although we do acknowledge that it is often
difficult to discern precisely how the Torah originated and exactly
what it dictates to us in many of life's situations, which is why we
prefer to speak of a quest for the Torah. Further, we believe in a
choosing God, a God who created a special role in His universe for
the people of Israel, though here, too, we refuse to interpret this in
too exclusive a manner. Our sense of justice—itself, we believe,
God-given—does not permit us to interpret the Chosen People
doctrine in a way that would exclude non-Jews from God's complete care and compassion.

Thus, the traditional triad of God, Torah, and Israel is accepted
by us in its traditional form. If we feel obliged to see the Torah as a
process as well as truth finally delivered in the past, and if we are
prepared to be reverentially agnostic regarding such doctrines as the
coming of the Messiah, that is because we view the tradition itself as
developing through the processes of human history. More fundamentally, we believe that the historical approach to the classical
Jewish sources is the result of the application of the human mind to
its search for truth. This very search, we affirm, is man's glory, a
tiny reflection of the divine light it is given for each generation to
reveal.

Perhaps it can all be summarized in this way: For the religious
naturalist, God does not speak at all. For the fundamentalists, He
has spoken so loudly, clearly, and unambiguously in the past that
all we need to do is to listen with our ancestor's ears. For the liberal
supernaturalist, *shema yisrael* is an injunction for each generation
of Jews to hear with its own ears what God has spoken in the past
and still speaks to His people today. The rest is not silence.

Notes

Notes to Lecture 1

1. For the history and resurgence of fundamentalism in Christianity see James Barr, *Fundamentalism* (London, 1977). One of the best defenses of Christian fundamentalism is J.L. Packer, *"Fundamentalism" and the Word of God* (London, 1958). The placing of quotation marks around the word in Packer's title is indicative of the tendency, to be observed on the Jewish scene as well, of fundamentalists to be uneasy with the term because of its pejorative connotations. I have discussed the topic in the Jewish context in: "World Jewish Fundamentalism," *Survey of Jewish Affairs 1987*, ed. William Frankel (London, 1988), pp.221–34. I used the term "liberal supernaturalism" to describe my theological position in the symposium *Varieties of Jewish Belief*, ed. Ira Eisenstein (New York, 1966), pp.109–22. The editor of this symposium observes that his purpose in assembling this collection of essays is to present the views of a diversified group of contemporary theologians. He goes on to remark:

> The second purpose (for the editor, at least, equally important) is to demonstrate the validity of the Reconstructionist contention that, in the Judaism of today and tomorrow, diversity of theologies must be recognized as both inevitable and desirable. . . .We have reason to hope that the encouragement of diverse conceptions of Jewish religion will stimulate creative thought, and help to render the tradition relevant, and even exciting.

It can be questioned whether the naturalists in the symposium, in view of their radical understanding of what God means, should better be seen as philosophers of Judaism rather than theologians. Cf. the too sweeping but not entirely irrelevant remarks of Bernard J. Heller, "The Modernist Revolt Against God," *Proceedings of the CCAR* 40 (1930):323–57.

> We need not fear the atheist and the skeptic. He has adopted a philosophy and has taken a definite position. He tells unequivocally what he believes or disbelieves and where he

stands. He calls a spade a spade. This makes it easy for us to comprehend his views and appraise them and point out what seem to be their inadequacies. It is, however, not so with the Jewish humanists. They vacillate and equivocate. They negate the cardinal affirmations and attitudes which religion demands and implies, and yet they persist in using the term "God."

Of course, this broadside, uttered over fifty years ago, begs the question. The religious naturalists have replied to this kind of critique by stating that, on the contrary, theirs is an attitude that religion demands or implies, and that theirs is the concept behind all the more sophisticated formulations of theism in the past. Yet this lecture has as its main aim to point to the religious inadequacy of the naturalist view.

2. The following two formulations, separated by several centuries, one by a great religious rationalist, the other by a determined religious antirationalist, can be quoted in this connection.

a) Maimonides, *Mishneh torah*, *Yesodey ha-torah* 1:1-3. It is the basis of all foundations and the pillar on which all wisdom rests to know that there is a Prime Being [*matzuy rishon*] who brought into being everything that exists and that all creatures in heaven and earth and between them only enjoy existence by virtue of His existence. If it could be imagined that He did not exist, then nothing else could have existed. But if it could be imagined that all beings other than He did not exist, He alone would still exist and He would not suffer cessation in their cessation. For all beings need Him but He, blessed be He, needs not a single one of them. It follows that His true nature [*amitato*] is unlike the nature of any of them [i.e. His is necessary being, whereas theirs is contingent].

b) Zevi Elimelech of Dinov (1785-1841), *Derekh pikkudekha* (Jerusalem, n.d.) no.25, p. 125. The nature of this command [to believe in God] is to believe in the heart in very truth that God exists. He, blessed be He, it is who, out of nothing, has brought all creatures into being. By His power and will, blessed be He, there has come into existence everything that was, is and will be and nothing exists except by His will and desire. His providence extends over all, in general and in particular, so that even the natural order is the result of His desire to use nature as the garment of His providence.

Maimonides believed that, as he goes on to say, belief in God's existence can be attained by the exercise of human reasoning. The Hasidic master relies on the truth as taught by the tradition and considers speculation harmful to faith, as he goes on to say in this passage. But, differ though they do on how faith is to be attained, the object of faith is conceived of by both in almost identical terms, insofar, at least, as personhood is concerned, though neither, of course, uses the term.

3. On the conflict between science and religion and the Darwin controversy there is, of course, a vast literature. Helpful summaries are provided in the older work by Andrew D. White, *A History of the Warfare of Science and Theology* (London and New York, 1897), pp.65ff. and in the more recent works Harold K. Schilling, *Science and Religion* (London, 1963); and D.C. Goodman, ed., *Science and Religious Belief* 1600–1900 (Dorchester, 1973). For the Marxist attack on theistic faith see James Collins, *God in Modern Philosophy* (London, 1960), pp.249–257; *K. Marx and F. Engels on Religion* (Moscow, 1957); David Elton Trueblood, "The Challenge of Dialectical Materialism," in *Philosophy of Religion* (London, 1957), chap. 12, pp.161–70. There is an immense literature on Freud and religious belief. Freud's own negative views on religion are contained chiefly in his *Totem and Taboo* (London, 1915); The *Future of an Illusion* (London, 1928); and *Moses and Monotheism* (London, 1939). Two helpful examinations of the way religious belief can face and overcome the Freudian critique are Leslie D. Weatherhead, *Psychology, Religion and Healing* (London, 1952); and H.L. Philp, *Freud and Religious Belief* (London, 1956).

4. For Tillich see his *Dynamics of Faith* (London, 1957). A severe critique of Tillich is found in the symposium *Religious Experience and Truth*, ed. Sidney Hook (Edinburgh, 1962). Here Howard W. Mintz (pp.254–60) faults Tillich's reductionism for lack of clarity and goes so far as to suggest that while the beliefs of a Billy Graham may not be true, they are more philosophically and logically tenable than those of Tillich. K. Nielson, in the same symposium (p.278) remarks that when Tillich equates belief in God with "ultimate concern" he makes the atheist, who also has "ultimate concern," into a theist. Nielson calls this "conversion by redefinition." See my book: *Faith* (London, 1968), p.22 n.2. "Conversion by redefinition" is precisely my accusation of the religious naturalists in this lecture. For the "Death of God" controversy, now somewhat old-hat, see the books of John Robinson, the Bishop of Woolwich, *Honest to God* (London, 1963); *The New Reformation* (London, 1965); and, with David L. Edwards, *The Honest to God Debate* (London, 1963). Cf. also Daniel C. Jenkins, *Guide to the*

Debate About God (London, 1966); C.D. Moule and others, *Faith, Fact, and Fantasy* (London, 1964). Don Cupitt, *The Sea of Faith: Christianity in Change* (London, 1984), is a more recent statement of religious naturalism and is open to the same critique on grounds of reductionism. It should be noted that Mordecai M. Kaplan anticipated all of these theories without receiving credit for them. Kaplan's classical work is *Judaism as a Civilization* (New York, 1936), but his main work on our theme is *The Meaning of God in Modern Jewish Religion* (New York, 1947). Cf. Kaplan's *Questions Jews Ask* (New York, 1958); and Ira Eisenstein (Kaplan's son-in-law and disciple), *Judaism Under Freedom* (New York, 1956). Also, Max Arzt, "Dr. Kaplan's Philosophy of Judaism," *Proceedings of the Rabbinical Assembly of America*, 5 (1938):195–219. In the same naturalistic vein from the Jewish side are Richard L. Rubenstein, *After Auschwitz* (Indianapolis, 1966); *idem., The Religious Imagination* (Indianapolis, 1968); and Harold M. Schulweis, *Evil and the Morality of God* (Cincinnati, 1984). Schulweis develops the novel idea of "predicate theology" but does not succeed in showing how one can have divine predicates without a divine subject and how such thinking qualifies as theology.

5. For a defense of the naturalistic view of prayer, see Eugene Kohn, "Prayer and the Modern Jew," *Proceedings of the Rabbinical Assembly of America*, 17 (1954):179–91. The same volume includes A.J. Heschel's "The Spirit of Prayer," pp.151–77, on the supernaturalist understanding. See the discussion of both papers, pp.198–217.

6. Recent accounts of the arguments for the existence of God and their refutation include Leszek Kolakowski, *Religion* (Oxford, 1982); E.C. Ewing, *Value and Reality: The Philosophical Case for Theism* (London, 1973; Richard Swinburne, *The Existence of God* (Oxford, 1979); and J.L. Mackie, *The Miracle of Theism: Arguments For and Against the Existence of God* (Oxford, 1982). An important question is whether it is logical to proceed inductively in building up the case for theism by an accumulation of the traditional arguments, each of which is inadequate in itself but which gains conviction when combined with the others. Swinburne (p.13 n.1) refers to Antony Flew, *God and Philosophy* (London, 1966), p.62f., who remarks that "if one leaky bucket will not hold water there is no reason to think that ten can." Swinburne, however, notes that arguments that are not deductively valid are often inductively strong, and if you put three weak arguments together you may often get a strong one. Thus if ten leaky buckets are placed together in such a way that the holes in one rest against the solid part of another, the ten buckets may hold water where one will not. There is a

comprehensive bibliography on the arguments in Paul Edwards and Arthur Pap, *A Modern Introduction to Philosophy* (Glencoe, Illinois and London, 1957), pp.619–21. On p.447 the argument is advanced that, in denying the existence of God, an atheist does not necessarily claim to know the answers to such questions as "What is the origin of life?" or "Where does the universe come from?" He merely rules out theological answers to these questions. The illustration is given: "If somebody asked me, 'Who killed Carlo Tresca?' I could answer, 'I don't know and it will probably never be discovered,' and I could then quite consistently add, 'But I know some people who certainly did not kill him—Julius Caesar or General Eisenhower or Bertrand Russell.' " This analogy is totally misleading. The man who says that he does not know who killed Carlo Tresca knows that Carlo Tresca was killed. The question "Who killed him?" is logically meaningful even though the answer may never be known. On the other hand, the atheist does not say that we may never know the origin of the universe but we know it was not brought into being by God. The atheist does not deny the solution; he denies the very question, since there is no middle ground between the statement that the universe just happened and the statement that it was created by God. Ultimately, it is a question of whether the search for meaning has any meaning.

7. Rabbi A.I. Kook, "The Pangs of Cleansing," in *Abraham Isaac Kook*, trans. Ben Zion Bokser (New York, Ramsey, Toronto, 1978), pp.261–69.

Atheism has a temporary legitimacy, for it is needed to purge away the aberrations that attach themselves to religious faith because of a deficiency in perception and in the divine service. This is its sole function in existence—to remove the *particular* images from the speculations concerning Him who is the *essence* of all life and the source of all thought. When this condition persists for a period of several generations, atheism necessarily presents itself as a specific cultural expression, to uproot the remembrance of God and all institutions of divine service. But to what uprooting did divine providence intend? [i.e. in allowing atheism to emerge as a philosophy] To uproot the dross that separates man from the truly divine light, and in the ruins wrought by atheism will the higher knowledge of God erect her Temple.

8. For a good account in English of the Maimonidean doctrine of divine *attributes*, see Isaac Husik, *A History of Medieval Jewish Philosophy* (Philadelphia, 1940), pp.261–66. The main discussion by Maimonides is in his *Guide* I:51–60.
9. See Bahya Ibn Pakudah, *Duties of the Heart*, trans. Moses Hyamson (Jerusalem and New York, 1978), vol. I, chap. 10, pp.98-123.
10. *Elimah rabbati* (Lemberg, 1881), I:10, p.4b.
11. For an account of the Kabbalistic doctrine of *En Sof* see I. Tishby, *Mishnat ha-zohar* (Jerusalem, 1957), vol. I, pp.98–130. Cf. Gershom G. Scholem, *Major Trends in Jewish Mysticism*, 3rd ed. (London, 1955), p.12:

The latter designation [*En Sof*] reveals the impersonal character of this aspect of the hidden God from the standpoint of man as clearly as, and perhaps even more clearly than, the others. It signifies "the infinite" as such; not, as has been frequently suggested, "He who is infinite" but "that which is infinite".

It should be noted, however, that among later Kabbalists the expression *En Sof, blessed be He* occurs frequently.
12. Joseph Albo, *Sefer ha-ikkarim*, trans. Isaac Husik (Philadelphia, 1946), vol. II, chap. 30, pp.96–97.
13. Richard Taylor, *Metaphysics* (Englewood Cliffs, 1963), pp.96-97. Taylor's is basically a new argument from design. If it just so happened that our minds have come together at random and the world just happened by chance, how can we use our minds in order to discover an order or design in the universe? Taylor's version of the argument from design has been assailed; see Barry Kogan, "Judaism and Contemporary Scientific Cosmology: Redesigning the Design Argument," in *Creation and the End of Days: Judaism and Scientific Cosmology*, ed. David Novak and Norbert Samuelson (Lanham, New York, and London, 1981), pp.97–155. I do not quote Taylor's as an irrefutable argument but as an indication that the relentless search for proof for the existence of God is for the God who endows human reasoning with its significance, not a blind force which, by definition, has no mind.
14. *Magen va-ḥerev*, ed. S. Simonsohn (Jerusalem, 1960), part II, chap. 4, pp.25–27.
15. See Isaac b. Sheshet Perfet, *Responsa Ribash*, ed. I.H. Daiches (New York, 1964), no. 157. Abraham Abulafia seems to have been the

first critic to compare the Sefirotic doctrine to Christian beliefs about the Trinity; see Moshe Idel, *Kabbalah: New Perspectives* (New Haven and London, 1988), p.xii and notes.

16. Michael Wyschogrod, "A New Stage in Jewish-Christian Dialogue," *Judaism*, 31 (1982):355–65.

17. See the sources cited in my article "Attitudes Towards Christianity in the Halakhah" in *Gevurat haromah (Jewish Studies Offered at the Eightieth Birthday of Rabbi Moses Cyrus Weiler)* (Jerusalem, 1987), pp.XVII-XXXI.

18. Huxley's coinage of the term agnosticism is described in a famous passage:

> When I reached intellectual maturity, and began to ask myself whether I was an atheist, a theist, or a pantheist; a materialist or an idealist; a Christian or a freethinker, I found that the more I learned and reflected, the less ready was the answer until at last I came to the conclusion that I had neither art nor part with any of these denominations, except the last. The one thing in which most of these good people were agreed was the one thing in which I differed from them. They were quite sure they had attained a certain "gnosis" — had more or less successfully solved the problem of existence; while I was quite sure that I had not, and had a pretty strong conviction that the problem was insoluble. [T.H. Huxley, *Collected Essays*, vol. 5, (London, 1893–94) pp.239-40]

19. John Stuart Mill, *Three Essays in Religion* (London, 1874).

20. E.S. Brightman, *The Problem of God* (New York, 1930).

21. Charles Hartshorne, *Man's Vision of God* (New York, 1941).

22. Saadiah Gaon, *The Book of Beliefs and Opinions*, trans. Samuel Rosenblatt (New Haven, 1948), II:13, p.134.

23. Thomas of Aquinas, *Summa Theologica*, part I, quest.25, 4.

24. Gersonides, *Milḥamot*, III:6. See Harry Slonimsky, *Essays* (Cincinnati, 1967). Slonimsky has developed a limited God theology on the basis of midrashic statements. There is no doubt that a surface reading of both the Bible and the rabbinic literature give the impression of a God who needs man to help Him in His struggle against that which is simply "given" and not of His making.

25. The best statement of the free-will defense of theism is that of John Hick, *Evil and the God of Love* (London, 1966). Hick develops the argument that the existence of evil makes the universe into an arena in

which man, by freely choosing the good, makes the good his own for all eternity. See Roland Puccetti, "The Loving God—Some Observations on John Hick's *Evil and the God of Love*," *Religious Studies*, II (1967):255–68. Puccetti argues against Hick that there is evil in the universe which can in no way contribute to human moral advance—the suffering of little children, for instance. Hick defends his views in "God, Evil and Mystery," *op. cit.*,539–46. An apparent random element in nature is essential, for if it were always possible to discover the teleological necessity of each kind of suffering this would interfere with man's free choice.

> The contingencies of the world process are genuine; though the existence of the whole process, with its contingencies, represents a divine creative act, the purpose of which is to make it possible for finite creatures to inhabit an autonomous world in which their creator is not involuntarily evident and in which, accordingly, their moral and spiritual nature may freely develop.

See on this Richard Swinburne, *Existence of God*, pp.200–24. On the Jewish side see L. Carmel, "The Problem of Evil: The Jewish Synthesis," *Proceedings of the Association of Orthodox Jewish Scientists*, I (1966):92–100. See also in the same volume, G.N. Schlesinger, "Divine Benevolence" pp.101–103, and Schlesinger's "Suffering and Evil," in *Contemporary Philosophy of Religion*, ed. Steven M. Cahn and David Shatz (Oxford, 1982), pp.25–31.

26. The best study of the Lurianic doctrine is I. Tishby, *Torat ha-ra ve-ha-kelipah be-kabbalat ha-ari* (Jerusalem, 1942).

27. *op. cit.*, p.346.

28. See my translation of Dov Baer Schneersohn, *Kuntres ha-hitpa-alut, Tract on Ecstasy* (London, 1963) and my study *Seeker of Unity* (London, 1966), for an account of this doctrine.

29. See the letters of anathema against the Hasidim in E. Zweifal, *Shalom al yisrael* (Zhitomer, 1868–9), vol.II, pp.37–60; and in M. Wilensky, *Hasidim u-mitnaggedim* (Jerusalem, 1970), vol. I, pp.187–90.

Notes to Lecture 2

1. This is discussed in the Talmud, *Bava Batra* 15a.

2. Moses Maimonides, Commentary to the Mishnah, *Sanhedrin* 10:1.

3. For the Maimonidean attempt (*Guide* III) to discover reasons for the mitzvot see Y. Heinemann, *Taamey ha-mitzvot be-sifrut yisrael* (Jerusalem, 1949) vol. I. Maimonides' critic, Shem Tov Ibn Shem Tov, in his *Sefer ha-emunot* (Ferara, 1556, photocopy edition, Jerusalem, 1969), writes:

> And when the Rabbi [Maimonides] comes to provide reasons for the commandments, the truth be told, no one will discover that any mitzvah is to be carried out for its own end. Either it is for the purpose of nullifying nonsensical opinions, as are [for Maimonides] all the laws concerning idolatry and its worship, the sacrificial system, the Temple and its vessels and those who minister therein, and to affirm God's unity; or for the purpose of controlling the appetites, as are the forbidden foods and sexual relationships and other mitzvot; or it is for the purpose of improving the character, as are charity, tithing, the poor man's gifts, and the laws of damages and monetary claims; or for the purpose of remembering the creation of the world and the unity of God. [I: chap. 1, p.7a]

Ibn Shem Tov himself favors the Kabbalistic view that the mitzvot have a theurgic effect, each exerting an influence on the Sefirotic realm. Similarly, Isaac of Acre, in his *Meirat eynayim*, ed. H.A. Erlanger (Jerusalem, 1975), writes:

> Although the words of the Guide for the Perplexed refine the mind and direct the intellect aright, bringing those who understand his ideas correctly to a comprehension of the Creator. . .yet in connection with the reasons for the mitzvot he said nothing at all adequate but only as one who tries to push away an adversary with a straw. [p.203]

4. *Shabbat*: 23a.

5. Commentary to Deut. 34: 1. Spinoza, *Tractatus Theologico-politicus* (Hamburg, 1670), quotes Ibn Ezra's brief comments in chapter eight and concludes that the Pentateuch is a composite work compiled in the days of Ezra. Of the numerous works on the Higher Criticism reference can be made to J.W. Colenso, *The Pentateuch and the Book of Joshua Critically Examined* (London, 1862–1879); S.R. Driver, *Introduction to the Old Testament* (Edinburgh, 1891); W. Robertson Smith, *The Old Testament in the Jewish Church* (Edinburgh, 1881); A. Bentzen, *An Introduction to the Books of the Old*

Testament (London, 1946); George Fohrer, *Introduction to the Old Testament* (London, 1968); A.S. Peake, ed., *The People and the Book* (Oxford, 1925); H. Wheeler Robinson, ed., *Record and Revelation* (Oxford, 1938); and H.H. Rowley, ed., *The Old Testament and Modern Study* (Oxford, 1958). Books by Jewish scholars include Umberto Cassuto, *The Documentary Hypothesis*, 3rd ed., trans. I. Abrahams (Jerusalem, 1959); *idem, From Adam to Noah* (Jerusalem, 1959); *idem, From Noah to Abraham* (Jerusalem, 1959); *idem, The Book of Exodus* (Jerusalem, 1959); and Yehezkel Kaufmann, *The Religion of Israel*, trans. and abridged by Moshe Greenberg (Chicago, 1960). Kaufmann observes of the detection of three sources in the law codes of the Pentateuch:

> Several of the conclusions of this theory may be considered assured. To this category belongs the analysis of the three primary sources — JE, P, and D — with their laws and narrative framework. The source JE is manifestly composed of parallel accounts, even though their unraveling cannot always be accomplished with certainty. The tripartite separation is clearest in the legal material. There are three legal corpora, differing from one another in their general style and juristic terminology, containing parallel and at times contradictory laws. These differences were recognized by early tradition and gave rise to harmonistic exegesis which is one of the features of rabbinic midrash. Only by accepting midrash as the plain sense of the text can the presence of separate legal compilations be denied. [p.156]

Nahum M. Sarna, *Understanding Genesis* (New York, 1966); and *idem, Exploring Exodus* (New York, 1986), are attempts, on the whole very successful, at demonstrating how the acceptance to some extent, at least, of critical views need not be incompatible with the traditional understanding of the Torah. Two useful works on textual criticism are Ernst Würthwein, *The Text of the Old Testament* (Oxford, 1957); and J. Weingreen, *Introduction to the Critical Study of the Text of the Hebrew Bible* (Oxford, 1982).

6. *Orot ha-kodesh*, ed. D. Cohen (Jerusalem, 1938), part V, pp.19-22. Other Orthodox Jewish thinkers who accept the theory of evolution as compatible with the Torah are J.H. Hertz, *Pentateuch and Haftorahs* (London, 1960), pp. 194–95; and I. Epstein, *The Faith of Judaism* (London, 1954), pp.194–208.

7. Nahman Krochmal, *Moreh nevukhey ha-zeman*, ed. S. Rawido-wicz (Berlin, 1924), Introduction, p.5.

8. Commentary to Isaiah 40:1. Dr. Hertz, *op. cit.*, pp.941–42, is prepared to discuss objectively the question of whether the book of Isaiah is a unity:

> The question can be considered dispassionately. It touches no dogma, or any religious principle in Judaism; and, moreover, does not materially affect the understanding of the prophecies, or of the human conditions of the Jewish people that they have in view.

9. *Sanhedrin* 99a.

10. See, for example, Joel Roth, *The Halakhic Process: A Systematic Analysis* (New York, 1986).

> If one is so inclined, one may reformulate the *Grundnorm* in the light of modern scholarship as follows. The document called the Torah embodies the word and the will of God, which it behooves man to obey, as mediated through the agency of J, E, P, and D, and is, therefore, authoritative. An alternative possible formulation might be: The document called the Torah embodies the constitution promulgated by J, E, P, and D, which it behooves man to obey, and is, therefore, authoritative. [p.10]

Roth, to be sure, speaks only of the legal system. As he remarks:

> Thus, it follows on one important level that the halakhic system qua system is independent of any considerations of the accuracy of the historical claims of its basic norm. Whether or not it is "true" that the Torah embodies the word and will of God is of great historical and theological significance, but of no legal significance. Even if one has traced the origins of the Torah to documents called J, E, P, and D, he may have uncovered the historical sources of the legal norms but he has in no way abrogated the *Grundnorm* of the halakhic system, which is presupposed by the system. As any number of observant scholars can attest, the system continues to function on the basis of its presupposed *Grundnorm* regardless of the contentions that the historical claims of the *Grundnorm* may be inaccurate. [p.9]

But while it is true that one can accept the *Grundnorm* as true from the legal point of view even if it is not "true" from the theological, it is hard to see why Roth's "observant scholars" should accept a legal "truth" based on a theological "error" and, if they do, why they are not being schizophrenic.

11. I have discussed the "Jacobs Affair" at length in my recently published *Helping With Inquiries: An Autobiography* (London, 1989), chap.9, pp.134ff.

12. M. Friedländer, *The Jewish Religion* (London, 1900), pp.46–138.

13. J. H. Hertz, *op. cit.* See especially the lengthy note on Leviticus, pp.554–63.

14. R. Samuel b. Meir (c.1085-c.1174) in his Commentary to Exod. 13:9. On the development of tefillin and other rituals see Samuel S. Cohon, *Essays in Jewish Theology* (Cincinnati, 1987), pp.335–66.

15. Exod. 23:19; 34:26; Deut. 14:21.

16. Ezek. 44:31.

17. (Oxford, 1984)

18. *Maharal* of Prague, *Tiferet yisrael* (London, 1955), Introduction, pp.1–3.

19. Especially in the field of bioethics the attempt to rely solely on the standard halakhic norms is fraught with danger. See for the attempt Immanuel Jakobovits, *Jewish Medical Ethics* (New York, 1975); J. David Bleich, *Judaism and Healing: Halakhic Perspectives* (New York, 1981); Fred Rosner and J. David Bleich, eds., *Jewish Bioethics* (New York, 1979). For a more balanced halakhic attitude, see David M. Feldman, *Health and Medicine in the Jewish Tradition* (New York, 1986) and *idem., Marital Relations, Birth Control and Abortion in Jewish Law* (New York, 1971); and for a critique of the "pan-halakhic" approach, Elliot N. Dorff, "Modern Medicine and Jewish Values," *Conservative Judaism*, 11 (Summer, 1988):73–80. On the general question of how Jewish law is seen today by representatives of the different schools of thought, see the symposium "Halakhah, Authority, and the Future of Judaism," *Judaism* 29 (Winter, 1980):4-l09.

20. *Berakhot* 31b.

21. *Maharal* of Prague, *Tiferet yisrael*, chap.2, pp.10–12.

22. *Midrash Tanhuma*, ed. Buber, *Tazria*, 7.

23. *Bava Batra* 10a.

24. *Midrash Tanhuma*, ed. Buber, *Tazria*, 7.

Notes to Lecture 3

1. See Jacob B. Agus, *Modern Philosophies of Judaism* (New York, 1941), pp.5–10.

2. For Halevi's qualitative views, see the standard edition of the *Kuzari* (Vilna, 1906), and, in English, Hartwig Hirschfeld's translation from the Arabic, *Kitab al khazari* (London, 1931), especially I:31–42 (Hirschfeld, pp.41–43); I:102–103 (Hirschfeld, pp.64–65); and V:20, Fourth Principle (Hirschfeld, p.254). For prophecy as confined to the native Jew and impossible even for the righteous proselyte, see I:115 (Hirschfeld, pp.69–70). For Halevi's famous description of Israel as "the heart of the nations," see II:36–44 (Hirschfeld, pp.95–96). Cf. *Sefer ha-kozari*, ed. Yehudah Ibn-Shmuel Kaufman (Tel Aviv, 1973), where some of the Maskilim are taken to task for dubbing Halevi's views "racist." Kaufman writes:

> R. Judah Halevi sees the whole human family as a single organism, in which the people of Israel have the function of the heart. How can this be termed "hyper-nationalism"? To the extent that the heart is the seat of faith, of love, fear and joy, of attachment to God, to the extent that this is bound up with the art of religious faith, this heart sustains the whole body including the soul residing in the brain. All human history involves the quest for God. When the people of Israel sought and found Him, having the merit of hearing God's voice and when Israel's prophets reached their elevated stage of revelation, was all this only for themselves or was it not for the sake of the whole human race?. . .Was it not R. Judah Halevi who explained Israel's exile as a mission to the nations to prepare them for the realization of the vision? This is the secret of the Exile, God's secret. When the family of nations will attain to a most elevated unity to become a family consisting only of heart, a tree of which the taste of the bark and the fruit will be the same. This is the aim of "the holy history of mankind." [n.21, pp.30–31]

This defense, cogent though it is in general, does not allow us to deny that Halevi sees Israel as superior in essence to the nations, albeit superior only in spiritual endowment.

3. See R. Shneur Zalman of Liady, *Tanya* (Vilna, 1930), trans. Zalman I. Posner (London, 1973), chap.2. Some "qualitative" Jewish interpreters of the doctrine have gone so far as to suggest that there are physical differences between Jews and Gentiles. See, for example, Eli-

jah b. Abraham of Smyrna, *Midrash talpiot* (Warsaw, 1875), 12, who remarks that Jews, according to one opinion, have only 32 teeth while Gentiles have 33 but that otherwise the only distinguishing mark of Jews is the sign of circumcision. According to this source, God did not make Jews physically different from Gentiles in any other way for two reasons. First, if Jews and Gentiles were too different, it would encourage a dualistic belief, that one god created Jews, another Gentiles. Secondly, it would not have been fair to converts to Judaism if they had a different bodily form from that of other Jews. The well-known commentator, Israel Lipschütz, in his *Tiferet yisrael* (var. eds.) to the Mishnah, *Avot* 6:10, believes that the facial features of Jews are different from those of Gentiles, that there is a special Jewish face:

> This is why a Jew has many more commandments than a Gentile since his soul is hewn from a most elevated Source and this can be discerned in the form of the face, different from the face of other human beings. . . .This is a most wondrous phenomenon. However, the difference in appearance of the face is due to the fact that the face is the window of the soul. There are to be discerned the qualities of wisdom and of folly; of courage and of anxiety; of anger and of pride; of humility and of love and so on. With regard to a Jew it can be detected that his soul derives from a unique Source higher than that from which the souls of other human beings are derived. [n.157]

4. Saadiah Gaon, *Beliefs and Opinions*, trans. Samuel Rosenblatt (New Haven, 1948), III:7, p.158.

5. *Betzah* 25b. In reality this statement is also "qualitative" but in reverse. Cf. Hayyim Ivn Atar, *Or ha-hayyim* (var. eds.) to Exod. 18:21. Gentiles can be superior in wisdom to Jews: witness Jethro, who advised Moses how to organize his affairs. God did not choose Israel because there are more wise men among the Israelites than there are among other peoples. The choice was solely an act of divine grace and due to the merits of the patriarchs.

6. *Avot* 3:14. Israel Lipschütz, in *Tiferet yisrael*, to this Mishnah lists a number of benefactors of mankind from the non-Jewish world to demonstrate that God "chooses" others as well as Jews to fulfill His purposes. Lipschütz mentions Drake who brought the potato to Europe, Jenner who discovered vaccination against disease, Reuchlin who defended the Talmud, and Guttenberg who invented printing.

7. On this see the observations by Harry M. Orlinsky, *Essays in Biblical Culture and Biblical Translation* (New York, 1974), p.80.

8. Gen. 10.

9. Meir Simhah Kahan, *Meshekh hokhmah* (Jerusalem, n.d.) *Shemot*, to Exod. 4:22, p.44.

10. See the sources in *Encyclopedia talmudit*, s.v. *Ben noah*, vol. 3, pp.348–62.

11. *Tosefta, Sanhedrin* 13:2. The later term "saints of the nations of the world" is in Maimonides, *Mishnah torah, Melakhim* 8:11 and in the commentary to the Mishnah of R. Obadiah Bertinoro, *Sanhedrin* 10:2.

12. *Shabbat* 68b.

13. Solomon Schechter, "The Dogmas of Judaism" in *Studies in Judaism* (Philadelphia, 1945), vol. I, pp.147–81; the comment about the atheist is on p.156.

14. Maimonides, commentary to the Mishnah, *Sanhedrin* 10:1, *Ḥelek*. See Schechter's essay, *op. cit.*, for the vexed question of whether there are dogmas in Judaism and my discussion with a bibliography in *Principles of the Jewish Faith*, rev. ed. (Northvale, N.J. and London, 1988), pp.1–32.

15. See, for example, Michael Rosenak, *Commandments and Concerns: Jewish Religious Education in Secular Society* (Philadelphia, 1987), with particular reference to the state of Israel, and Jonathan Sacks, *Traditional Alternatives: Orthodoxy and the Future of the Jewish People* (London, 1989), with a comprehensive bibliography of recent Orthodox thought on the subject, pp.255–63. See also the paper I delivered to the Roman Catholic group, the 10th Downside Symposium, "Judaism and Membership," *Church Membership and Intercommunion*, ed. John Kent and Robert Murray, S.J. (London, 1973), pp.141–53, in which I tried to summarize this subject briefly:

> To sum up, and if the comparison is not too banal, Judaism is like the philosophy of a club with a particular purpose over and above the purely social. The club's founder members all belong to one family as do the majority of its present-day membership, but membership is open to all who accept the club's particular philosophy. Full membership is granted to these after an initiation ceremony. The club's constitution contains a large number of strict rules. Some of the members adhere lovingly to these and tend to look askance at those members who disregard the rules. Other members press for a revision of the rules and still others quietly neglect some of them. Once a person has become a

member he is held to be a member for life even if he no longer
pays his dues, attends meetings or obeys any of the rules. He is a
member in absentia and will always be welcomed back. It is only
when he joins a club which has a contrary philosophy that his
fellow-members consider membership to have lapsed.
[pp.152–53]

16. See, for example, *Guide* III:27.
17. *Sanhedrin* 4:5.
18. Even the fundamentalist ArtScroll Series admits this. In the commentary to the Mishnah *Sanhedrin* (New York, 1987), p.74, the commentator remarks, "Other versions do not specify the destruction or
preservation of a soul in Israel. This latter approach would seem to be
supported by the fact that Adam was not a Jew." Unfortunately, that
note continues, "However, it is possible that once the Jewish people
were chosen to fulfill the primary role of mankind by accepting and
following the Torah, the validity of this lesson applies only to them"
[*sic*].
19. *Berakhot* 17a.
20. See for the literature on Maimonides' views, Jacob I. Dienstag,
*Eschatology in Maimonidean Thought: Messianism, Resurrection and
the World to Come* (New York, 1983).
21. Nahmanides, *Torat ha-adam*, in *The Collected Writings of
Nahmanides*, ed. H.D. Chavel (Jerusalem, 1963), [Heb.], vol. II,
pp.309f.
22. Maimonides, *Mishneh torah*, *Teshuvah*, chap. 8.
23. *idem.* Commentary to the Mishnah, *Sanhedrin* 10:1.
24. *idem. Mishneh torah*, *Melakhim* 12:4.
25. *Avot* 4:17.
26. See M.H. Luzzatto, *Kelah pithey hokhmah* (Jerusalem, 1961),
no.4, p.7a.
27. For this idea see the essay "On Immortality and the Soul" in *The
Aryeh Kaplan Reader* (New York, 1983), pp.175–183.
28. In some circles there is a gratuitous assumption that modern Jews
tend to reject the doctrine of the hereafter. See, for example, Henry
Abramovitch, "Death," in *Contemporary Jewish Religious Thought*,
ed. Arthur A. Cohen and Paul Mendes-Flohr (New York, 1987), who
writes: "Orthodox Judaism still clings staunchly to such notions, but
other strands of modern Jewish thought are uncomfortable with the
notion of the afterlife." [p.132] This is an odd assessment of the views
of the non-Orthodox who have prayers for the repose of the soul in their

various liturgies. Cf. the pamphlet *Emet ve-emunah: Statement of Principles of Conservative Judaism* (New York, 1988), which has a section on Eschatology (pp.28–30). After stating that some followers of Conservative Judaism take the doctrine of the soul's immortality literally, enabling them to confront death and the death of their loved ones with courage and equanimity, the pamphlet goes on to say that others have a more figurative understanding:

The doctrine of the immortality of the soul affirms that our identities and our ability to touch other people and society does not end with the physical death of our bodies. Great personalities from the beginning of history remain potent influences in the world. On a more personal level our friends and the members of our families who are gone are still palpably alive for us today.

It would be a useful exercise to trace when modern Jewish thinkers began to substitute the idea of living on in our works or our children for the full-blooded belief in personal immortality. It is exceedingly odd that in all the contemporary Jewish discussions on theodicy in general and on the Holocaust in particular, there is hardly any reference to the doctrine of the hereafter.

29. A. C. Ewing, *Value and Reality* (London, 1973), p. 95.

30. Joseph Albo, *Sefer ha-ikkarim*, ed. Isaac Husik (Philadelphia, 1946), book IV, chap.32, p.322.

31. Leszek Kolakowski, *Religion* (Oxford, 1982), pp.157–58.

DATE DUE

HIGHSMITH   # 45220